Lillian Too's
Chinese Wisdom

Dedication

To Jenn and her dad, my husband, with love.

Lillian Too's
Chinese Wisdom

SPIRITUAL MAGIC FOR EVERYDAY LIVING

FRIEDMAN/FAIRFAX
PUBLISHERS

A FRIEDMAN/FAIRFAX book
Please visit our website: www.metrobooks.com

This edition published by arrangement with Cico Books Ltd
First published in Great Britain in 2001 by Cico Books Ltd
32 Great Sutton Street
London EC1V 0NB
(020) 7253 7960

M 10 9 8 7 6 5 4 3 2 1

ISBN 1-5866-3163-2

Designed by Sue Miller
Illustrators: Sam Wilson, Emily Hare, Sarah Perkins
Reproduction by Alliance Graphics   Printed in Italy

1 3 5 7 9 10 8 6 4 2

Distributed by Sterling Publishing Company, Inc.
387 Park Avenue South
New York, NY 10016

Distributed in Canada by Sterling Publishing
Canadian Manda Group
One Atlantic Avenue, Suite 105
Toronto, Ontario, Canada M6K 3E7

Distributed in Australia by
Capricorn Link (Australia) Pty Ltd.
P.O. Box 6651
Baulkham Hills, Business Centre, NSW 2153, Australia

Lillian Too welcomes you to:
* **Her website at www.lillian-too.com**
* **The first and most popular online feng shui magazine at www.wofs.com**
* **The largest Ecommerce site on feng shui at www.fsmegamall.com**
* **Her jewellery site at www.lilliantoojewellery.com**
* **Her free feng shui greeting cards site at www.fsgreetings.com**
And to fellow Buddhists to meet her guru at www.lamazopa.com

Many thanks to Cindy Richards for so cleverly conceptualizing this book, which was such a joy to write,
and to Liz Dean and Mandy Greenfield for their brilliant editing. Together, they have transformed my
simple manuscript into an intensely beautiful, meaningful book ... I feel very fulfilled and very grateful.

contents

Introduction

Part two: Earth Luck

Part three: Mankind Luck

Chinese wisdom and the
three great teachings

Chinese wisdom is a captivating blend of the three sources of energy that embellish our existence: heaven, earth, and man – tien, ti, and ren. Some call this luck; others call it chi. It can be viewed as the breath, the essence, or the life force of existence. It can manifest itself either physically or spiritually, and it can subsist at different planes of consciousness.

Heaven luck is associated with deities and states of bliss. Paradise is described differently under each of the three great teachings that make up the composite of Chinese thought – Confucianism, Taoism, and Buddhism. Earth luck concerns the living environment, while mankind luck is the common force that links the two. Heaven and earth represent the two metaphysical forces that manifest as "divine magic", while heaven, earth, and man collectively signify the trinity of energy that shapes the living world.

Opposite: To the Chinese, the Buddha represents an enlightened being who has transcended the cyclic karma of births and rebirths. Karma manifests as heaven luck – the circumstances we are born into. Feng shui, symbolized here by the Pa Kua, represents the luck of the environment or earth. Mankind luck is what one creates out of earth and heaven luck. Together, they symbolize the trinity of luck.

There are multiple dimensions in Chinese wisdom and a wealth of practices and rituals for improving every aspect of the human condition. Enhancement takes place on the material, physical, or spiritual plane, so that we can think of Chinese wisdom as a cumulative assortment of practical signposts in the journey of life, ensuring that we live long, live well, and live wisely.

*T*here are meditative exercises for attaining a state of mind that promises happiness – and even the bliss of spiritual attainment. At its most profound, Chinese wisdom can engender a transcendental realization that will make you understand the true nature of life, living, and existence. At its most practical and worldly, it pledges wealth and material comfort.

THE THREE GREAT TEACHINGS

1 Confucianism
Wisdom of the Ancients

Confucianism provides an ethical backdrop of doctrines that emphasize order. It advocates rigid codes of behavior, stresses the importance of the family unit, and is unashamedly despotic.

The doctrines of this particular philosophy have their roots in the *I Ching*, or *Book of Changes* (see p. 36), whose texts and commentary – while generally regarded as metaphorical descriptions of oracles – contain principles for living. Here is the wisdom of the ancients, wisdom that may seem excessively dogmatic at first glance, yet is said to contain the key to unlocking a great many of the "secrets" of existence. The *I Ching* and its sixty-four hexagrams are as intellectually challenging today as they have been throughout their 3,000 years of existence.

2 Taoism
A Duality of Opposites

Taoist wisdom offers some penetrating insights into the way of the cosmos. It explains everything within the world as a duality of opposites, with one object or concept giving existence to the other. In this way, Taoist thought presents a series of teachings that reveal "the way back to the Source," and it is both spiritual and worldly.

3 *Buddhism*
The Path to Enlightenment

Buddhist philosophy is completely spiritual and its teachings speak not merely of this life but of thousands of lifetimes, lived not only in the realm of human existence but also in other realms. In all, there are Six Realms of Existence (see p. 80), which represent the "hell"

The philosopher Confucius is probably the best known of China's sages. He spent a lifetime studying the I Ching *and his commentaries are highly revered. They form the basis of a set of codes, or principles, for living.*

"Taoist philosophy and Buddhist meditative techniques can soothe the fierce currents of existence and help you sail around submerged rocks and obstacles that suddenly block your path."

and "heaven" of conventional terminology. Buddhist thought embodies the path to enlightenment and offers a rich tapestry of contemplative practices, rules that define virtuous actions and moral behavior and, most important of all, the development of a good heart, which manifests itself in an attitude of spontaneous compassion toward all living beings. Its meditative rituals promise the bliss of heaven beyond this life, known as "enlightenment" – a state of mind that is said to combine compassion with wisdom, and one that all practising Buddhists strive to attain.

This is Mahayana Buddhism, the Buddhist teaching that was traditionally practised in China, and is still practised by Chinese Buddhists throughout the world today. Its most popular deity is the stunningly compassionate Goddess of Mercy, the beautiful Kuan Yin. Today Kuan Yin has millions of devotees and her mantra, *Om mani peh meh hone,* is chanted throughout the world by all those who meditate on her image. Not many non-Buddhists realize that the Indian manifestation of Kuan Yin is the Lord of Compassion, Avalokiteshvara, while the Tibetan manifestation is the Buddha Chenresig, also referred to as the Buddha of Compassion. His Holiness the Dalai Lama is believed by Tibetan Buddhists to be the earthly manifestation of this most kind and compassionate Buddha.

A PATH OF DISCOVERY

*M*y purpose in writing this book is to share a way of living that incorporates some of the fascinating practices and profound wisdom extracted from the three teachings that make up my cultural heritage. I am convinced that these bite-sized morsels can offer real help to you, the reader, as you navigate your way through the uncharted waters of life's destiny.

I know that Taoist philosophy and Buddhist meditative techniques can soothe the fierce currents of existence and help you sail around submerged rocks and obstacles that suddenly block your path, thereby helping you to avoid dangers that lurk on your road to happiness. There is depth and magic in the secret knowledge of the three teachings, which can be a source of great comfort and life-changing optimism.

You will find – as I did – that the content and substance of Chinese wisdom does not necessarily become more difficult as you go deeper. The development of wisdom is a flow, just as much as it is a contemplative examination. Realizations and superior insights arise in no particular order as you read and enjoy the knowledge that unfolds. You will find certain aspects more appealing and seductive than others. It depends on where you are in your present awareness of life. You may want to dwell longer on some passages, while skimming swiftly through other parts that seemingly hold little relevance for you at this time. No single tenet or practice is deeper or more shallow than another. Basic beginner concepts can be as profoundly illuminating as apparently more advanced ideas. Even the fun of using divination methods and practising Taoist rituals can hold out the promise of mysterious outcomes.

It is a good idea to let your impressions and judgments flow freely. Enjoy questioning the reasoning behind ideas and mentally challenge them as you move from one topic to the next. This strengthens your quest for accurate and useful knowledge. More importantly, it should open your eyes and engage your interest sufficiently to make you want to investigate further.

RITUALS FOR TRANSFORMING YOUR LIFE

*I*ncluded in the following pages are user-friendly explanations of the popular methods of fortune-telling and destiny analysis. These are based on dates of birth, facial features, and palm lines. Oracles and divinations are very much a part of the Chinese psyche, due to the belief that antidotes and cures can be used to enhance good predictions, as well as to reduce the impact of predicted misfortunes (some of which can even be avoided). What you need is to be forewarned. Thus bad heaven luck can be tempered by rituals related to the manipulation of energies in your living space.

Bad heaven luck can also be counteracted by using transcendental purification ceremonies, or by following powerful meditative practices. Exercises of the mind can transform even dire circumstances into deeply pleasurable sensations – and result from gaining experiential insights, although these require vigorous discipline and frequent practice. Meditation can bring blissful realizations, so that life becomes joyous and meaningful, despite physical or material discomforts.

Such contemplative exercises may be enhanced and taken further by reciting mantras and performing mystical mudras, or hand gestures. Mantras invoke a heightened sense of awareness and are part of spiritual practices that focus on raising the mind higher – they

"Be prepared to move with the natural flow and order of things in the cosmos. Keep an open mind: swim with the tide, not against it. Let the profound concepts of the ancients come alive, become meaningful, seem easy. Let it make a real difference to your life."

can be extremely powerful. Meanwhile physical exercises, such as tai chi kung, which resemble graceful, ritualistic dancing, delve into the more profound aspects of physical energy development.

Mental or physical, these rituals aim to raise the chi that facilitates the attainment of expanded states of consciousness. This leads to an inner stillness that creates situations conducive to the transformation of perceptions and attitudes. Many of the aids to progress – yogic breathing, chi kung, and other physical exercises, mantras, mudras, diets, health foods, sexual encounters, and so on – have already been discussed in publications written during the past decade.

There are also rituals that extend into everyday living and which can become elaborate, colorful occasions. Festivals are replete with gestures rich in symbolic meaning. Symbolism pervades Chinese thought at every level of attainment, and gods or deities who personify some material aspiration or other are very much a part of the Chinese cultural landscape. Gods of Wealth, for instance, abound in the Chinese pantheon (see p. 22).

The Taoist concepts of yin and yang and the Five Elements define the world's mutually supportive and destructive activities. There are methods of eating, exercising, and resting that are collectively based on these concepts, while special herbal cures, unique health foods and soups, and extraordinary massage techniques offer easy ways to achieve healthy living and longevity.

Contained in the pages of this book are selected morsels of the finest of Chinese wisdom, classified in terms of heaven, earth, and mankind luck. Come travel with me on a path of discovery into my background and my heritage. It might give you some answers to your unspoken questions and lead you into the spiritual high ground of matchless bliss, or it might make your life richer, more abundant, healthier, and less stressful. To each of you will come your own expectations.

Be prepared to move with the natural flow and order of things in the cosmos. Keep an open mind: swim with the tide, not against it. Let the profound concepts of the ancients come alive, become meaningful, seem easy. Let it make a real difference to your life.

llars of the tao

ormless aspect of the Tao,
cosmos as a multitude of
one is to comprehend the

naterial things and become
earances. Perception of life
– it leads to the meaningless!

To neglect the child is to ... naterial world and focus only on intangibles – again, leading to the meaningless.

"The origin of the cosmos is the eternal mother... To grasp the mother is to know the child; to know the child is to hold fast to the mother. Then life becomes secure."

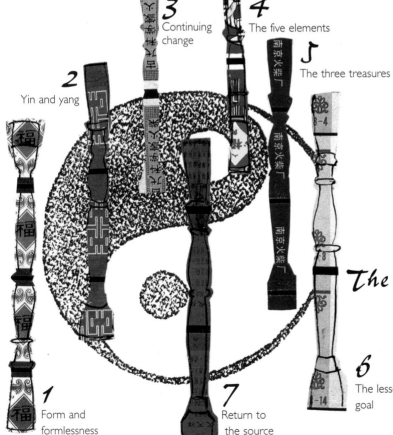

2 Yin and yang

3 Continuing change

4 The five elements

5 The three treasures

1 Form and formlessness

7 Return to the source

6 The lesser goal

The Seven Pillars of the Tao

1 *The first pillar*
The Concept of Form and Formlessness

This idea can be likened to a mother and child. To embrace both mother and child is to welcome the totality of the cosmos and to understand that spirit and matter are one and here and beyond are one. This concept of form and formlessness is the first fundamental pillar of the Tao, which is at once seamless, intangible, and void, yet simultaneously everything that our senses perceive in the here and now. The concept is very similar to the Buddhist view of Emptiness, which states that form is void and void is form. To grasp this fully, you need to cultivate the meditation of stillness. Understanding this basic tenet of Taoism requires many hours of silent contemplation.

The life-cycle of the flower is a symbol of constant birth and re-birth, the third pillar of the Tao. The bud and the full bloom also encapsulate the idea of yin and yang, the second pillar, in that they represent the tension of opposites without which the universe cannot exist.

2 *The second pillar*
The Concept of Yin and Yang

Taoism explains that the existence of all things is one manifesting two complementary forms. Thus, everything in the cosmos contains shift-

ing forms that operate through the interaction of polar forces named yin and yang. These forces, or energies, should be clearly recognized as two sides of the same coin, so that what is perceived at any one moment is merely one perception of the same thing, which may be a yin perception or a yang perception.

In this way, yin and yang manifest, for example, as the sunless and sunny sides of a mountain. The shaded face of a mountain is viewed as its Receptive aspect. The bright, sunny face of the mountain is viewed as the Creative and dynamic aspect. The Receptive and Creative together give form to the void, and void to the form, of the mountain. Neither can exist without the other. There can be no notion of sunlight unless we understand shade (that is, where there is no sunlight).

Correspondingly, there can be no light (yang) without dark (yin); no day without night; no hills without valleys; no dynamism without stillness; no plus without minus; and no male without female.

You can apply this same reasoning to all manifestations of phenomena. Both yin and yang – representing the polarity of forces, energy, and chi – must always be present. One is never found in isolation from the other – simply because one gives existence to the other.

Pure yang energy always contains the seed of yin; and pure yin always contains the seed of yang. At a mundane level, you can imagine there being a little bit of male in all women and a little bit of female in all men! It is only through the varying interactions of yin and yang that all objects of the phenomena world differ from each other. Thus, every person, every space, and every possible outcome differs, because its mixture of yin and yang differs. If you contemplate this, you will realize that the combinations of yin and yang are infinite.

Yin and yang should always be in harmony. Harmony disappears when an imbalance of any kind occurs, which causes the phenomena to disintegrate and take on other shapes and forms. This explains the ups and downs of existence; good luck and bad luck; growth and decay; life and death. The practice of the Tao helps you to maintain a perfect balance of yin and yang, and to accept with equanimity when this balance is disturbed. When something is broken, you merely start again – there is never a permanent end. This leads us on to the third concept.

Pure yang energy always contains seeds of yin, and pure yin always contains seeds of yang.

THE FIVE ELEMENTS ARE DESCRIBED AS:

● Metal: the category of endurance, strength, and unbendingness.
● Wood: the category of growth, fruition, and eventual decay and death.
● Water: the category of regularity, flow, and persistence.
● Fire: the category of ambition, change, and power.
● Earth: the category of the receptive, the supportive, and the matriarch.

3 *The third pillar*
The Concept of Continuing Change

In the whole universe, the only thing that is unchanging is change itself. Everything is continually altering and in a state of flux. Nothing stays permanently the same: every second, every minute, every hour of existence, everything in the universe continually changes. This fundamental truth is the very core of existence. Yet this dynamic – this constant flurry of activity – does not lead to chaos, so the ever-changing remains forever unchanged! Although this may seem like a contradiction, in understanding this you will begin to understand the true way of the Tao.

If you view all phenomena as a series of cyclical patterns, then you will notice that change takes place in the regularity of day becoming night and then becoming day again. There seems to be one endless cycle of change, and this has been the case throughout beginningless time. The same phenomenon of change applies to the seasons, as summer moves into winter and back to summer again. The manifestations of cosmic phenomena are transformed by the regular cycles and patterns. Thus the earth is orbited by the moon; and the earth itself orbits around the sun. It has been like this forever. When you apply this same theory to humans, you can see the cycle as being one of birth, growth, decay, and death. It is inexorable that we are born only to grow, blossom into adulthood, and then become old, until eventually we die.

Buddhists refer to this cycle of birth, death, and rebirth as the karmic cycle of life and give it the name *samsara*. Their practices are aimed at attaining liberation from samsara, and prayers are made to the Buddhas for blessings to achieve such liberation.

Taoism, on the other hand, while deeply spiritual, does not require spiritual devotion and practices of a religious nature. Rather, the Tao advocates that it is sufficient to perceive, contemplate, and meditate upon the majestic and cyclical nature of transformations. We view these transformations with awe, and even a certain amount of reverence, and then we meditate upon their smooth and effortless progression. This enables us to achieve perfect balance within the whole. Thus, the Taoist sage never tries to get the universe to accommodate him, but instead develops himself and his mind to accommodate harmoniously the workings of the universe. In this way, the individual submerges selfish urges, attachments, and ego and flows effortlessly back to the source of all existence.

I find such profound wisdom awesome indeed; yet, to be perfectly frank, I only half-understand it. I am certain that my interpretation is correct, but I strongly believe that a genuine understanding relies upon the help of a spiritual master. Understanding will bring further insights, which will require divine blessing from a higher being – a "god" presence. Perhaps this is why Buddhists seeking a perfect understanding of life depend on the guidance of a guru.

4 The fourth pillar
The Five Elements

In seeking to explain the changes in the cosmos, Taoism looks more to science than to the divine. Early Taoist scholars, it seemed, scientifically sought to explain the interactions of nature's forces in terms not only of yin and yang polarity, but also of five broad categories of mutually productive and destructive activity. In Chinese, these five forces, or *wu hsing,* are more recently translated as the Five Elements or, more accurately, the "five activities categorized by five elements."

The Productive Cycle

Everything in the universe falls into one of these five categories, and each of the elements has a yin or yang aspect, a positive or negative dimension, and a small or large manifestation. It is said that one of the greatest tests of a Taoist adept is the depth of his or her appreciation of the interactions of these Five Elements and what impact they have upon, and how they indicate the nature of all phenomena and all aspects of change. Thus, all forms of astrology and divination depend on an interpretation of the Five Elements for a reading to be accurate.

In the Productive Cycle of elements, wood produces fire, fire produces earth, earth produces metal, and metal produces water in a never-ending cycle.

Effective feng shui practice is almost completely dependent on an understanding of how the Five Elements interact within the home. A positive interaction creates a peaceful, auspicious environment. So, to engender a smooth flow along the Taoist path, the Five Elements of your surroundings should be conducive to harmony and balance.

The Three Treasures of the Tao are the semen, the breath, and the spirit. A full appreciation of these treasures signifies an advanced understanding of Taoism.

The attainment of a state of bliss is the sixth pillar of the Tao.

5 *The fifth pillar*
The Three Treasures

Deeper Tao practice requires an appreciation of the Three Treasures of existence, described as the semen, the breath, and the spirit. Each of these treasures is said to have a cosmic counterpart, thereby making a total of six interacting treasures. It is through the creation, nourishment, and interplay of these treasures that incredible "magical" abilities are attained, which prepare the way for a return to the Source (see below). This interpretation of Taoism bears similarities to the secret teachings of Buddha, which are known as tantric Buddhism – an advanced philosophy that promises the quick path to enlightenment. I can only guess that the divine magic of Taoist practices is similar to the remarkable yogic powers that we hear about as the attainment of Indian holy men and Tibetan high lamas. It is impossible to be definitive about this, however – such teachings are mostly secret, and transmissions require the guidance of a holy guru or lama.

The practice of the Three Treasures requires the supervision of a competent teacher and involves numerous vows and preparatory exercises. To attempt it on your own, without the help of a highly qualified guru, is to risk extreme danger to your mind and health. For this reason, Taoist books seldom dwell on this subject, and it is not something you can learn from books or by watching video tapes. Mention is made of it here merely to inform you, the reader, of the existence of this highest path to eternal bliss. If you are lucky enough to find a qualified teacher who is happy to take you on as a student, then you can consider yourself most fortunate indeed.

6 *The sixth pillar*
The Attainment of the Lesser Goal

Since achieving the ultimate goal – return to the Source – is so difficult, many Taoists are perfectly happy to aim at a lesser goal: that of attaining increasingly profound realizations, or intuitive insights, into the true nature of existence. These realizations are almost always accompanied by sensations of intense bliss.

In addition, these realizations cause a deepening of wisdom and generate a wonderful feeling of joy and peace with the world, because they offer such a profound understanding of life's meaning that they engender a wealth of beneficial side-effects, such as experiencing a feeling of youthful invigoration, excellent health, and physical vigor, which will enable you to attain a long and happy life. This seems to be the promise of Taoist practice.

Taoist longevity is always accompanied by radiant health, as well as a joyous tranquillity that makes every moment of life seem worth living. It is a higher state of happiness than the sort that comes only from material possessions. Instead, this type of joy wells up from deep within us. When you achieve it, you will never again feel bored or frustrated, never again react negatively to loss, bereavement, anxiety or fear. As a result, you will become such an agreeable person that everyone will feel your aura of inner happiness.

When you meet advanced Taoist adepts, even those who are reclusive, it is impossible to be indifferent to their merry disposition because their happiness is so contagious. Often they also possess extraordinary skills in writing poetry, in art, and in the practice of physical exercises such as chi kung. There is much to be said in favor of the cultivation of inner stillness that can lead to such realizations.

The Chinese Immortal Lao Tzu is widely acknowledged as the founder of Taosim, although his name literally means "the old sage." He embodies the return to the Source, which is the seventh pillar of Taoist wisdom.

7 *The seventh pillar*
Return to the Source

The ultimate goal of Taoist practice takes us into the realms of life after death, back to the Source, which can mean different things to different practitioners. One definition of the Source is the attainment of immortality, which we can imagine as a spiritual being who lives in a spiritual realm. Legend describes the paradise of the Queen of the West – a seemingly inaccessible part of Earth, depicted as a place where everything is available in abundance.

Another, perhaps more profound, definition of the Source is a goal so high that it transcends all other goals conceived by humans throughout time. Mere words, it is said, cannot describe the state of being back at the Source. The attainment of the ultimate is thus an experience so exalted – a wisdom so divine – that it transcends all existence.

The Chinese pantheon of
gods and their origins

A noticeable feature of Chinese religious worship is the veneration of deities from the "three teachings" – Taoism, Buddhism, and Confucianism. This combination of religious figures is reflected in the placing together in full splendor of the "gods" of the three doctrines – Lao Tzu, Shakyamuni, and Confucius, with seemingly little regard for religious boundaries.

*T*he Buddhas of the Chinese pantheon all have their "counterparts" in the Buddhist traditions of Tibet. It is, however, important to differentiate between Buddhas, Taoist "gods," canonized heroes and symbolic deities that represent aspirations such as longevity, wealth and marriage.

The Chinese have always sought spiritual satisfaction and, until the coming of Buddhism to China in the second century AD, this need for spiritual sustenance manifested itself in ancestor worship, as well as in the worship of deities that signified their worldly aspirations. Many of these gods were important personalities from Chinese mythology or heroes from legendary tales of past times, who had been deified after their deaths.

MYTHOLOGICAL GODS

Chinese mythology is colorful and reflects a version of the creation of the universe that is fundamentally different from the stories of the Christian Old Testament. The "Creator" was Pang Ku, whose birth is described as the fusion of yin and yang forces. Pang Ku took eighteen years to create order out of a chaotic universe.

He assembled heaven and earth, the sun, the moon, and the stars and, as he created, he grew taller and taller by the year until, upon his demise, his head became the mountains, his breath became the wind, his voice became the thunder, and his limbs became the four quarters of the earth. These were later named the cardinal directions. His blood became the earth's rivers, his skin became the plants and trees, his sweat became the rain, while his teeth and bones

Opposite: Unlike the Western creation story in which the world was made in seven days, according to Chinese legend, it took the mythological god, Pang Ku, eighteen years to create order from chaos – and the earth as we know it today.

became the gold and precious stones of the earth. The tiny creatures that fed on his rotting carcass became human beings! The origin of man, according to Chinese mythology, thus presents a rather humbling view of us humans.

After Pang Ku, it is written, came the mythical kings, the most prominent of whom were Fu Hsi, who invented elements of the *I Ching* and introduced civilized living, and Emperor Huang Ti, who is referred to as the Yellow Emperor. Three mediocre rulers followed, and collectively these kings came to be known as China's legendary Five Rulers. They figure prominently in Chinese cultural history. Mythology ended with the last of these emperors, although today these legendary rulers continue to be worshipped.

Then there are the "gods" – deified generals taken from the period of the Three Kingdoms in the third century AD, the most famous and popular of whom was Kuan Kung (see p. 27), who is worshipped as the God of War and Wealth. In addition, the Chinese also worshipped nature – the mountains, the rivers, the sun, the moon, the stars, and even rocks were identified as "holy."

The legendary Emperor Fu Hsi is highly acclaimed as a wise sage and ruler. He is remembered for his discoveries, many of which have been directly incorporated into the texts of the original I Ching.

In many ways, this reflected an innate desire to appease the unknown. Worship of the Moon Goddess or the Wind Dragon King, for instance, represented a form of safeguard and also protection against calamities such as floods, typhoons, and earthquakes. Equilibrium with the forces of nature was deemed to be achieved by reverence to, and worship of, some form of deity associated with objects that represented nature.

REASON VERSUS LOGIC

Balance with nature and with the "gods" was believed to create order, harmony, and happiness. This seemed to reflect the Chinese everyday philosophy of life. The basic tenet was to live and behave reasonably, if not necessarily logically. Living reasonably necessitated a reverence for the personages that "ruled" the spiritual world. These in turn would ensure that the mountains would not fall upon them, that the winds would not blow excessively strongly, that the earth would not open and swallow them up into the dark abyss of hell.

The subtle difference between reason and logic is apparent in the Chinese attitude toward many things. Thus the emperor's law was deemed logical for ruling the country, but emperors deemed to be great were those who administered the law with reason. Alongside this, laws were supposed to be strict in and of themselves but should nevertheless be applied with leniency.

The purpose of worship reflected people's preference for reason over logic in the order of their lives. Chinese spiritual worship takes place both at home and also in the temple and, until the advent of Buddhism, many colorful legends dominated the relationship of the Chinese family to "heaven."

Kuan Yin can be seen as a Buddhist Madonna. She is the Goddess of Mercy and she signifies the essence of compassion and loving kindness for all sentient beings.

This cemented the widely held conviction that the trinity of forces within the universe comprised heaven, earth and man. Heaven was appeased at temples, supplemented by worship at home shrines; earth was appeased through a reverence for nature; and man was appeased by living in harmonious interface with heaven and earth.

INCORPORATING THE BUDDHAS

With the introduction of Buddhism into China came the Buddhas and Bodhisattvas – a pantheon of gods described not so much as deities but as "enlightened beings." The Buddhas had Indian origins and, reflecting the Chinese attitude of expediency, Buddhist deities were simply "added" to the existing collection of gods.

The Yellow Emperor, about whom many legendary tales abound.

Therefore, if you were to enter some of the old Buddhist temples in villages and small towns in China, you would discover that they are not solely Buddhist, since there are other "gods" inside the temples as well. Usually displayed in the main hall of a temple is a large Buddha statue, depicting Buddha Shakyamuni (the historical Buddha) or Buddha Amitabha (the Buddha of Longevity), but in the inner courtyards and halls will be a variety of other "gods". Following is an introduction to some of the more popular deities that feature strongly in the Chinese tradition.

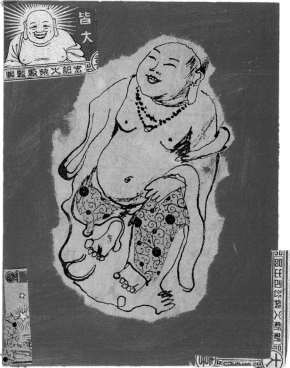

The Laughing Buddha, the most popular of Buddhist deities.

One of the Eighteen Arhats, or monks, who brought Buddhism to China.

1 *Symbol of joy*
The Buddha of Happiness or the Laughing Buddha

The Laughing Buddha is said to be a manifestation of the future Buddha of Loving Kindness – the Maitreya Buddha. He is usually depicted as being fat, with a wide smile. He has a big belly and carries a large bag in which he is said to store all the problems and sorrows of the world. His image in the home brings great joy, and it is believed that by merely looking at his fat, happy face you will feel joyous. The Laughing Buddha is a popular image of good fortune, whose symbolic presence in any home or office brings humility, happiness, and good relationships.

2 *Dharma protectors*
The Four Heavenly Kings

These are the guardians of heaven, and Buddhists regard them as holy beings who are *dharma* protectors (that is, they ensure that the doctrines and teachings of Buddha do not get sullied or corrupted). The Four Heavenly Kings look after bad luck or negative occurrences deriving from the four directions.

3 *The Goddess of Mercy*
Kuan Yin

Kuan Yin is probably the most popular deity in the Chinese pantheon. One legend (see p. 88) describes her as a princess who lived during the Zhou Dynasty (1122–221 BC). Buddhists regard her as a manifestation of the Hindu male deity Avalokiteshvara, while in Tibetan Buddhism she is the Buddha of Compassion, Chenresig, and in Japan she is known as Canon. She is usually shown seated and with the Buddha Amitabha or flanked by two other goddesses, Pu Hsien and Wen Shu.

4 *Master yogis*
The Eighteen Arhats

Usually depicted as meditation hermits, these monks continue to be revered as master yogis, who were largely responsible for spreading Buddhism into China.

5 *The Taoist God of literature and God of Examinations*
Wenchang and KuiShing

The God of Literature is the deified Tang Dynasty scholar Wenchang, whose brilliance so impressed the emperor that he had him canonized after his death. The God of Examinations is KuiShing, who is usually shown holding a pen and standing on a tortoise. Scholars worship the God of Examinations and it is believed that his image in the study room brings good fortune for them.

6 *The Taoist God of War and Wealth*
Kuan Kung

Kuan Kung is one of the famous trio of generals who were sworn blood-brothers during the period of the Three Kingdoms. The other two were Li Bei and Zhang Fei. Kuan Kung has a red face and a fierce countenance, which is said to send all evil spirits and people with bad intentions scuttling away in fright. He is the ultimate protector, and he is present in many Chinese households. Because of his character and his exemplary show of loyalty, Kuan Kung epitomizes all the good qualities, and he is thus the patron god of many professions. He is often shown standing in full fighting regalia or seated reading the Spring and Autumn Annals.

7 *Savior of souls*
Kshitigarbha or Di Chang Wang

Kshitigarbha is the overlord of hell and is higher than the ten kings of hell. He carries a staff with six rings in one hand and a jewel in the other hand. One tap of the staff opens the gates of hell, while the jewel emits brightness that lights up the whole realm. He is the god who delivers souls from hell.

● There are several hundred lesser-known gods who take care of other areas and aspirations. Different villages and towns also have their own local deities.

Kuan Kung, the general who lived during the period of the Three Kingdoms, is regarded today as the patron saint of police and criminal gangs. He is also regarded as a powerful God of Wealth, who bestows speculative luck.

MULTI-DEITIES

● In China, religious worship has mingled so much with superstitious belief and spiritual meditative practices that many modern Chinese — including those who were neither born in China nor live there now — are sometimes confused by the seemingly endless number of gods. But for those who have made a serious study of the origins of Chinese deities, it is not difficult to separate the truly religious deities, from the non-religious.

The eight trigrams and their
symbolic overtones

The eight primary trigrams are the roots of the *I Ching's* sixty-four hexagrams. Each trigram comprises combinations of three straight lines, which are unbroken (yang) or broken (yin). They illustrate the trinity of man, earth, and heaven. The lowest line is that of earth, the center line symbolizes man, and the top line represents heaven. In this way, the trigrams encapsulate the hierarchy of the universe.

"The starting point in understanding the eight trigrams is to learn their major symbolic associations."

The Later Heaven yang Pa Kua with the eight primary trigrams.

The most significant attribute of the trigrams is that they intermingle and, in so doing, create new and constantly changing aspects to their relationships. This intermingling is expressed as heaven and earth determining the directions. Heaven is Chien, the ultimate yang trigram, which is also symbolic of the leader and the patriarch. Earth is Kun, the ultimate yin trigram, which also signifies the matriarch. Both of these trigrams signify the union of father and mother, the male and female aspects of human beings.

The trigrams also express the unity of mountain and lake. Mountain is Ken, which means keeping still; lake is Tui, which symbolizes joy.

A third relationship speaks of thunder and wind arousing each other. Thunder is Chen, while the wind is the trigram Sun. The symbolism of Chen is the eldest son, while that of Sun is the eldest daughter.

The final relationship between the trigrams indicates the surprising non-compatibility of water and fire. Water is Kan, while fire is Li.

Each of these eight trigrams has additional meanings at a gross and subtle level. Extensive references are made to these meanings in almost all branches of fortune-telling and divination. The key to understanding events and their outcome is to examine the interaction between the trigrams, as they exist within a hexagram.

Thus, in each six-line hexagram, there are two sets of double trigrams, the first being the obvious bottom three lines and the top three lines. In addition, there are also the hidden or "nuclear" trigrams (see p. 36), which comprise the three lines formed by the second to fourth lines and by the third to fifth lines. These are usually counted from the bottom up.

DECODING THE TRIGRAMS

Analyzing the lines of the trigrams is an acquired skill that cannot be perfected overnight. The cryptic secrets of the *I Ching* are yielded up slowly – and then only to those whose study is genuine and reverential. Trigrams offer valuable clues not only in and of themselves, but also in their interaction with one another. In addition, trigrams have symbolic attributes that relate to their associations with compass directions, elements, members of the family, and parts of the internal physical body. Trigrams also have a soft and a dark aspect, and possess both yin and yang attributes. Attempting to comprehend fully their meanings is what makes the *I Ching* such a study in complexity. It also explains why there are so many different interpretations of the trigrams. Nevertheless, when understood, they do yield highly potent secrets. In the physical realm, extensions of the trigrams' meanings can often bring about auspicious outcomes.

For instance, there are formulas that enable you to calculate your lucky trigram. Armed with this valuable piece of information, you can "activate" that part of the space that corresponds to that trigram. How to categorize space in terms of trigrams depends on yet another formula. Many of these formulas interact with each other, and their collective potency, when correctly assessed, can be quite awesome.

1 Chien

2 Kun

3 Chen

4 Sun

5 Kan

6 Li

7 Ken

8 Tui

INTERPRETING THE TRIGRAMS

Trigram	1 Chien	2 Kun	3 Chen	4 Sun	5 Kan	6 Li	7 Ken	8 Tui
Meaning	heaven	earth	arousing	gentle	abysmal	clinging	mountain	lake
Family	father	mother	1st son	1st daughter	2nd son	2nd daughter	3rd son	3rd daughter
Image	male	female	thunder	wind	winter	summer	stillness	joy
Element	metal	earth	wood	wood	water	fire	earth	metal
EHA/LHA*	S/NW	N/SW	NE/E	SW/SE	W/N	E/S	NW/NE	SE/W
Animal	horse	cow	dragon	cock	–	–	–	sheep

* EHA = Early Heaven arrangement of the trigrams around the Pa Kua; LHA = Later Heaven arrangement.

"The Book of Changes contains the Tao of the holy sages. Therefore the superior man, when confronted with a decision, consults the Changes...

In speaking, let us be guided by its judgments. In action, let us be guided by its changes. In building our dwellings, let us be guided by its images. In seeking advice, let us be guided by its pronouncements."

RITUAL DIVINATION TECHNIQUES

Divination techniques that involve the *I Ching* should not be confused with fortune-telling or astrology. The *I Ching* is a dynamic force which, when stimulated, has the ability to penetrate all situations under heaven. Otherwise, it stays quiet, has no consciousness, and no action; it does not move. When it is consulted through any of the ritual divination techniques involving yarrow stalks or coins, the *I Ching* becomes stimulated and penetrates the depths of a problem, focusing like a laser beam on the particular circumstance described. It does not tell you the story of your life or destiny, as laid out in an astrological birth chart.

Thus, the *Book of Changes* is an oracle that dispenses advice on a specific situation or circumstance. It predicts possible outcomes, lays out options and offers advice on the basis of "right" and "wrong," "good" and "bad." It presents judgments and commentaries, and it describes results through the use of metaphorical statements and images. In the words of the book, and the imagery of its lines, lie the answers to many questions – you are able to reach all depths and to grasp the seed of all things; you can even penetrate the wills of those who walk the earth.

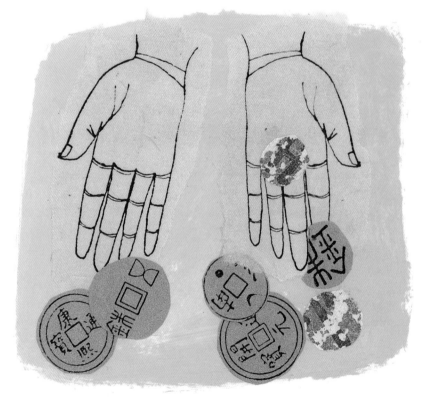

Answers offered by the *I Ching* may be profound and shrouded in so many layers of imagery that their meaning often escapes the uninitiated. Those unfamiliar with the underlying philosophy of the *Book of Changes*, approaching it in only a superficial manner, will find it impossible to penetrate the veil of the words to reach the advice hidden inside the words and imagery. So, consulting the *I Ching* is something to be taken seriously – it is not a "fun" thing.

This immediately becomes obvious in the answers given when the *I Ching* oracle is used in jest or disrespect. Indeed, often the book seems to take on a life of its own as it dispenses answers that chide those who questioned it. For instance, if you were to ask the same question over and over again, it is likely that the *I Ching* would either throw you a ridiculous, unintelligible answer or would simply say, "Ask and ask again – only an immature youth needs to speak thus!"

On the other hand, if you first clear your mind and then focus strongly on the question to which you seek an answer, then formulate your question clearly, setting out the problem as precisely as you can, you will have started to enter the ritual of divination.

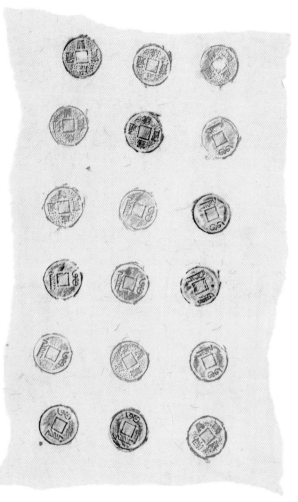

Chinese coins can be used for divination. The yang side of the coins has four characters which say "your luck has arrived," while the yin side has two characters. Coins are powerful symbols of prosperity luck.

Regardless of whether your question concerns something near or far, secret or profound, immediate, or some time away, the *I Ching* takes on the form of the oracle and an appropriate answer is usually given: one that is not difficult to comprehend. Often the situation at hand is so vividly and accurately described in terms of the parameters or personalities involved that it seems quite uncanny.

In many commentaries of the *I Ching*, its oracular nature has been stressed repeatedly. It is said that the *I Ching* discloses things that are hidden, describes affairs unknown even to the person consulting it and depicts all outcomes to possible courses of action or decisions. Scholars of the *Book of Changes* contend that the *I Ching* oracle is as applicable today as it was 3,000 years ago.

YIN AND YANG

To understand the meanings of the lines, it is useful to appreciate the dogmas that lay behind their creation. Thus, consider that in the beginning there were two primary forces, yin and yang, manifested in broken (--) and unbroken lines (–), representing darkness and light. These two forces then became four images through a process of doubling; these four images also correspond to the four seasons of the year. This is represented in linear form thus:

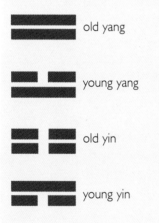

old yang

young yang

old yin

young yin

By adding a third line to the linear images, the eight trigrams arose. These determine good fortune and misfortune, and the two outcomes create the great field of action.

MASTERING THE RITUALS

*T*he divination rituals are not difficult to master. Essentially they involve throwing either yarrow stalks or coins to determine the hexagram that offers the solution to carefully worded questions. Constructing the appropriate hexagram is the easy part of the ritual. The challenging part is interpreting the hexagram created; reading the symbolism of the main trigrams and hidden "nuclear" trigrams; and understanding the predictions given in the changing lines. Finally, it depends on how good you are at interpreting the second hexagram that is created by the changing lines.

In understanding the messages of the *I Ching*, you also need to appreciate the nature of yang and yin lines. This difference can also be expressed in the way the coins or stalks fall, determining the kind of hexagram that gets constructed. Only once you have such knowledge can you obtain reliable answers from the *I Ching* oracle.

Those wishing to use the *I Ching* oracle should invest in a good translation of the book and engage in the serious practice of quiet meditation. This will encourage the ritual of divination to engage the mind in a focused fashion. The actual throwing of the coins or stalks is often less important in getting an accurate outcome than the intensity of concentration achieved during the consultation. Coins and stalks should be kept "pure" (that is, stored in velvet or silk) and used only for the purpose of consulting the oracle.

USING THE COIN ORACLE

The coin oracle uses three old Chinese coins with a yang and a yin side. Each time the coins fall, they will display one of the following combinations. An "x" indicates a changing line.

1 Three yang sides, which makes it an old yang line about to change into a yin line, so three yang sides indicate a changing line indicated thus ▬ **x**

2 Three yin sides, which makes it an old yin line about to change into a yang line, so three yin sides will make it a changing line indicated thus ▬ ▬ **x**

3 One yang and two yin sides, which makes it a young yang line, and this makes it an unbroken unchanging line indicated thus ▬

4 One yin and two yang sides, which makes it a young yin line, and this makes it a broken unchanging line indicated thus ▬ ▬

The coins are thrown six times and this constructs the six lines of the hexagram. Changing lines are also indicated by the way the coins fall. Once you have your hexagram, you are then able to consult the Book of Changes to study the hidden and unhidden messages of advice offered by the hexagram. When there are changing lines, a second hexagram is also created, which often represents either the predicted outcome to the question or additional options that might be pursued. See the table on page 37 to interpret your hexagram.

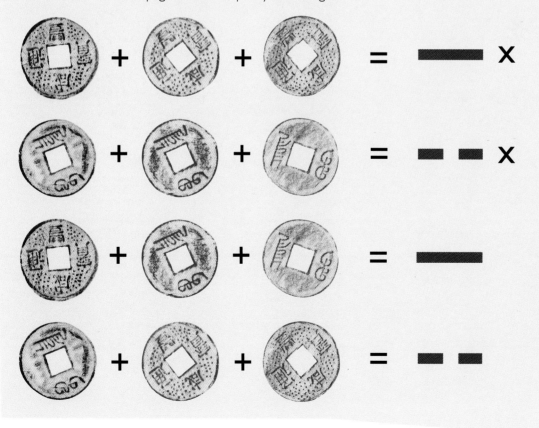

The sixty-four hexagrams of
space and time

"Looking up, we contemplate the signs of heaven.
Looking down, we examine the conditions of the earth.
We come then to know of the dark and the light...
Going back to the beginning of things
and pursuing them to the end,
we learn the lessons of birth and death.

The union of seed and power produces all things
and chi energy brings about change."

*T*he sixty-four hexagrams of the *I Ching* are built on the two fundamental elements of light and dark. The lines of the hexagrams are either at rest or in motion. When at rest, they build up the hexagram; when in motion, they break down the hexagram and transform it into a new one. These two simple processes contain the secrets of the *I Ching* and of life itself.

When a line is broken, it represents the dark, the earth, and the yielding; it signifies yin. When it is unbroken, it represents the light, heaven, and the unyielding; it signifies yang. But yin and yang lines can be at rest or in motion, reflecting all the nuances of a hexagram – inner, outer, and secret. At the most obvious level, interpretation of the hexagrams is based on the relationship of the two sets of trigrams that make up each one.

Each hexagram contains four trigrams: two upper and two lower ones. Each of these has an attribute, a symbol, and a characteristic. Each can also be related to one of the Five Elements and is either yin or yang. If we examine the anatomy of each hexagram, we can see the two sets of trigrams, as shown in the example given below.

THE HEXAGRAMS

● As we have seen, the hexagrams are created by doubling the eight trigrams in all their possible combinations. The trigrams have already been described in terms of their major symbolic associations (see p. 28). If you want to go deeper, I recommend that you investigate some of the more authoritative source books on the *I Ching*.

● The table opposite summarizes the formation of the sixty-four hexagrams, with the horizontal row forming the upper trigrams and the vertical row forming the lower trigrams. The resulting hexagram is given in the form of numbers, which are explained on pp. 38–41.

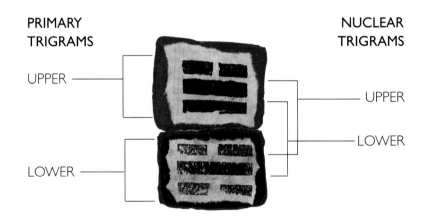

PRIMARY TRIGRAMS

NUCLEAR TRIGRAMS

UPPER

LOWER

UPPER

LOWER

The primary trigrams usually reveal the circumstances of the situation, while the nuclear trigrams reveal the hidden agendas and meanings. The latter sometimes provide very precise details for judging the nuances of predicted good or bad fortune. Sometimes, however, the advice is shrouded in incomprehensible metaphorical language. It is, therefore, best to use an authoritative translation of the *I Ching* if you wish to use it as an oracle. When consulting the *Book of Changes*, it is important to know the superficial and hidden meanings of the trigrams, since their combination is what makes up the hexagrams. It is the trigrams that give shape and meaning to the hexagrams, and the interactions of the trigrams create the hexagrams. Thus hexagrams express the state of rest and motion of any given circumstance.

The Book of Changes offers advice on when to be decisive and when to stay still and cultivate patience. It addresses outcomes and options that might otherwise have stayed hidden. Many of the strategies contained in the celebrated journal of warfare, Sun Tze's *Art of War*, focus on the absolute importance of timing, highlighting when it is wise to stay absolutely motionless, and when to spring into action.

Much of this ancient philosophy applies to today's world, where patience seems to be a forgotten virtue. In the mad rush to gain a competitive edge, an entire generation has grown up worshipping at the altar of speed and activity. They forget that sometimes it is just as prudent to do nothing, until circumstances are more conducive to action or time reveals what was previously unknown.

FORMATION OF THE 64 HEXAGRAMS

Trigrams	Chien	Chen	Kan	Ken	Kun	Sun	Li	Tui
Chien	1	34	5	26	11	9	14	43
Chen	25	51	3	27	24	42	21	17
Kan	6	40	29	4	7	59	64	47
Ken	33	62	39	52	15	53	56	31
Kun	12	16	8	23	2	20	35	45
Sun	44	32	48	18	46	57	50	26
Li	13	55	63	22	36	37	30	49
Tui	10	54	60	41	19	61	38	58

Each hexagram consists of two primary trigrams. Look up the trigrams on the horizontal and vertical axes respectively, then turn to pages 38–41 for a summary of the hexagram meaning.

1 Chien: the Creative brings success and blessings from heaven. Complete yang lines indicate benefits from perseverance. This is the hexagram of the patriarch. Heaven moves powerfully and with unceasing strength, and man can emulate this.

 2 Kun: the Receptive brings great success, which arises from the hard work of the matriarch. She has the greatness of character to bear all the hardships of the world. This hexagram indicates the strengthening of relationships.

 3 Chun: indicates difficult beginnings, but perseverance brings success. It advises planning and the need for good helpers.

 4 Meng: indicates the ignorance and folly of youth.

 5 Hsu: indicates a time for nourishment and hard work.

 6 Sung: indicates conflict, but sincerity will dissolve obstructions.

 7 Shih: indicates the army and the leader who expands his group of followers by being benevolent and persevering.

 8 Pi: symbolizes harmonious cooperation, a coming together of the parts to make the whole – union and merger. Proceed with caution, for too much hesitation brings misfortune.

 9 Siau Chu: rest and preparation – a taming of the small energies.

10 Lu: indicates a need to be careful and to step lightly, for there is danger of offending someone. The clever person is able to differentiate between wise and foolish, high and low, and carries him- or herself accordingly.

11 Tai: signifies peace and a time of good fortune. The small departs and the big arrives. So there is great success and luck.

12 Pi: here indicates stagnation: a time of poverty and difficulty.

13 Tung Jen: indicates cooperation among friends and siblings.

 14 Ta Yu: signifies great possessions and material wealth. There is glory, honor, and recognition. It is time to suppress evil and pursue virtue.

 15 Chien: here signifies a time to lie low and wait. There is great virtue in modesty.

 16 Yu: here signifies joyous enthusiasm and happiness. It is a good time to start new ventures and expand your resources.

 17 Sui: indicates that there is equal virtue in being a good follower and staying loyal to the leader. Thus can there be great success.

18 Ku: suggests the end of a bad period and the start of good times. Wait for three months and things will begin to improve. A time to cultivate virtue.

 19 Lin: signifies making an approach, giving a proposal. The hexagram advises you to proceed, as success lies around the corner.

 20 Kuan: signifies that it is better to wait than to take action. The winds bring only dust, so success has to be found in another place.

 21 Shih Ho: indicates quarrels, obstacles, and harsh words – this is a time to withdraw.

22 Pi: here indicates beauty and a decorative image, which may or may not have substance. Investigate and clarify.

 23 Po: signifies decay and grave misfortune, when one is exposed to harsh winds and much danger. It is better to postpone or delay your plans.

 24 Fu: signifies a return to better times after a bad harvest. Friends come back and everything becomes much easier.

 25 Wu Wang: indicates success coming from unexpected sources. It represents the triumph of innocence; you get noticed by important and influential people.

 26 Ta Chu: indicates great internal strength. It also signifies that you have a major task ahead of you, but that you will succeed – like heaven being found within the mountain.

 27 I: indicates nourishment and encourages you to continue to persevere, but to move with caution. The image is of thunder rolling at the foot of the mountain.

 28 Ta Kuo: indicates great excess. It is wise to cool down before proceeding.

 29 Kan: indicates a situation of danger that may lead to legal entanglements and great misfortune. It is best to withdraw before the water overflows.

30 Li: indicates intense brightness and sunlight – an unstable situation of excessive highs. There is too much yang energy; slow down.

31 Hsien: indicates energizing and also stimulation – the oracle says that to proceed is to attract good fortune, but there is need also for humility.

32 Heng: indicates duration and firmness. A situation of good omens.

33 Tun: indicates withdrawal. Better to offer victory to the enemy and live to fight another day. It is termed strategic withdrawal.

 34 Ta Chuang: suggests thunder in the sky, a loud heralding of power. All power and strength are indicated. It is certainly wise to be wary.

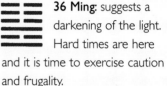 **35 Chin:** indicates a time of new beginnings, where there is initial progress in all directions, but there might be separations and setbacks. It is good to stay committed.

 36 Ming: suggests a darkening of the light. Hard times are here and it is time to exercise caution and frugality.

 37 Chia Jen: signifies a focus on the members of the family, which can also mean employees. The patriarch leads through speech, while the matriarch's perseverance benefits the family.

38 Kuei: means confrontation. Fire above the lake indicates conflict and opposition, so it is beneficial to identify who is for you and who is against you.

 39 Chien: indicates danger and difficulty caused by obstructions. Water above the mountain is a situation of grave danger. It is time for re-examination.

 40 Sieh: signifies deliverance from obstruction and blockages. Rain comes after a period of drought. This is a time for forgiveness and compassion.

41 Sun: represents decrease and signifies loss and disappointment. There is little profit to be had, so anger should be transformed into patience.

 42 I: represents increase and indicates gain, profits, and expansion. There are signs of advantages on the horizon, so proceed with confidence.

 43 Kuai: signifies the determination and resolution of a situation. The danger is not fully over, so it is wise to continue to be wary and humble.

 44 Kou: indicates new circumstances arising suddenly and without warning. The wind blows under the sky, bringing a woman of substance. Marry her – or hire her.

 45 Sui: indicates a lots of people all getting together to pay homage to a great man – a situation that suggests benefits of an unexpected nature.

 46 Sheng: signifies ascending good fortune. There is future promotion, advancement, and also wealth.

 47 Kun: indicates imprisonment or being hemmed in. There is oppression and liberation in this hexagram. Extreme measures are needed to survive and thrive.

 48 Ching: signifies the well that is the source of water – but it can also run dry. A situation of high risk is indicated here. Be careful.

 49 Ko: indicates an upheaval and a time of rebellion. Take care.

 50 Ting: the cauldron indicates an image of good fortune. There is great potential to build something mighty, so do persevere.

 51 Chen: signifies thunder, a loud noise, massive publicity – get ready to become famous in the four corners of the earth.

 52 Ken: signifies stillness, rest, a time of getting ready. Here the image is the mountain that houses many treasures.

 53 Chien: indicates a situation that is gradually improving. The image is that of a tree growing on a mountain – an auspicious symbol denoting growth.

 54 Kuei Mei: signifies an undertaking that leads to suffering and unhappiness. It denotes an error of judgment and advises a retraction.

 55 Feng: this symbolizes brilliance and prosperity – a great future. The image is of the blazing sun at noon, so there is an implied warning to be cautious, for a waning sun follows noontime brightness.

 56 Lu: means the wanderer. It suggests a lack of purpose.

 57 Sun: signifies the power of the wind, which scatters seeds far and wide.

 58 Tui: represents the lake doubled, signifying joyousness and success. It is especially beneficial for young women and girls.

 59 Huan: spells separation, but this leads to great things and meeting powerful patrons. Crossing the great waters will be beneficial.

 60 Chieh: signifies the limits established by your circumstances. The clever person devises ways of overcoming these limitations.

61 Chung Fu: signifies honesty and inner compassion, sincerity and confidence.

62 Siao Kuo: symbolizes small mistakes that can be overlooked. It is important to continue, but to do things slowly, taking one step at a time. Walking is to be preferred to running.

63 Chi Chi: signifies the completion of a project or quest. To continue with great success is hard and there is danger ahead, so it is wise to be wary.

64 Wei Chi: represents the state before completion, when concentration and hard work are required. This hexagram also signifies a beginning of sorts. The wise person is careful to work correctly just before completion.

● These are the sixty-four hexagrams and it is necessary to contemplate beyond their obvious images and meanings. For those of you whose interest has been aroused by this small and most inadequate summary, I strongly recommend that you seek out a Taoist master – as I did, many years ago. Explanations rendered face-to-face reveal nuances that go far beyond the scope of the written word.

Horoscopes:
the stems and branches

"Watch how things grow, fed by roots that find mineral sustenance from the earth, nurtured by water and brought into bloom by the warmth of sunshine."

The popular view of Chinese astrology is the categorization of the years according to twelve animals. These animals, in order, are: the Rat, the Ox, the Tiger, the Rabbit, the Dragon, the Snake, the Horse, the Sheep, the Monkey, the Rooster, the Dog, and the Boar. Many legends explain the choice of the animals included in the Chinese horoscope; one describes the selection of these animals by Buddha as a reward for their respectful presence during celebration prayers to mark his birthday.

Another story purports that the Heavenly Jade Emperor, bored with life in heaven, asked his courtiers to assemble twelve earthly animals for his amusement. The emperor was pleased with them, and therefore made each animal one of the earthly branches of his calendar.

A third version speaks of a competition organized by the King of Heaven, in which all the animals of the universe were to cross the fast-moving Lo River. The first twelve to reach the other side were selected to represent the years of the calendar. The order of appearance in the cycle is usually explained by their sequential appearance before the exalted personality who selected them.

There are also stories to explain the Rat being the first animal of the zodiac. Apparently the Rat did not run all the way to beat the rest. Instead, he hitched a ride on the back of the unsuspecting Ox and, just as they reached the finishing line, jumped off and landed in front of him. The fact that he was not censured for his craftiness, so the

# of fortune

story goes, reflects heaven's approval of those who use their head. I prefer to view the selection of animals in terms of ancient wisdom, particularly as it applied to the mainly agricultural and superstitious society of ancient China. Thus the Rat, being the all-important king during times of famine, comes first in the cycle because food is vital for survival. Being aggressive and clever, he is also deemed a yang animal. The slow-moving, hard-working Ox is made a yin animal. The festive fifth year – tumultuous and exciting – is given over to the Dragon, while the boisterous seventh year is deemed the Year of the Horse. The tenth year belongs to the proud Rooster, who struts around, while the twelfth year belongs to the slow, indolent Boar, and so on. The cycle always starts with the Rat and ends with the Boar. The twentieth century started with the Year of the Rat, while the year 2000 is the Year of the magnificent Dragon, which is followed by the Year of the Snake in 2001.

THE STEMS AND BRANCHES

The animals form the twelve earthly branches of the year. These twelve branches, together with the ten heavenly stems, make up a Chinese horoscope. In the annual lunar calendar of the sixty-year cycle, each of the stems features six times, while each of the branches features five times.

Under this system, each year has a name comprising two characters. One character refers to the stem of the year, while the other character refers to the branch.

THE NAMES OF THE 12 EARTHLY BRANCHES, OR YEARS:

TZU	= Rat = water
CH'OU	= Ox = earth
YIN	= Tiger = wood
MAO	= Rabbit = wood
CHEN	= Dragon = earth
SZU	= Snake = fire
WU	= Horse = fire
WEI	= Sheep = earth
SHEN	= Monkey = metal
YU	= Rooster = metal
HSU	= Dog = earth
HAI	= Boar = water

THE NAMES OF THE 10 HEAVENLY STEMS, OR ELEMENTS:

CHIA	= wood
YI	= wood
PING	= fire
TING	= fire
MOU	= earth
CHI	= earth
KEN	= metal
SIN	= metal
ZEN	= water
KWAY	= water

Horoscopes:
lunar birth-year calendars

HOW TO USE THE LUNAR BIRTH-YEAR TABLES

*U*se the following tables to determine the animal sign that rules your year of birth. This represents the earthly branch of your horoscope and offers wonderful insights into your character and personality. After determining the relevant animal, refer to any good Chinese horoscope guide, which will offer descriptions of the men and women who are born under the respective animal signs, their behavioral tendencies and also their personality characteristics.

Notice that each animal has a ruling element that does not change with the years. Thus, the Rat is considered to be of the water element, the Dragon of the earth element, the Horse fire, the Monkey metal, and so on. By themselves, the elements do not signify much. However, when matched with the element represented by the particular heavenly stem of your year of birth, this combination of elements becomes a potent additional indicator of your characteristic tendencies, both positive and negative.

The next stage in the analysis goes deeper, investigating what kind of Sheep, for example, you might be dealing with: a water Sheep, a metal Sheep, a fire Sheep, and so on. We have seen that in a sixty-year cycle, the Five Elements appear only once per animal year, so at this stage of the analysis there are already sixty different types of personalities!

After using the tables opposite to determine the two elements that represent your year of birth, you can then use these elements to determine your compatibility with the other animal signs.

LUNAR BIRTH-YEAR TABLES 1912–2004

Animal	Earthly branches	Calendar dates	Year name	Heavenly stem
RAT	water	Feb 18, 1912–Feb 5, 1913	Zen Tzu	water
OX	earth	Feb 6, 1913–Jan 25, 1914	Kway Chou	water
TIGER	wood	Jan 26, 1914–Feb 13, 1915	Chia Yin	wood
RABBIT	wood	Feb 14, 1915–Feb 2, 1916	Yi Mao	wood
DRAGON	earth	Feb 3, 1916–Jan 22, 1917	Ping Ch'en	fire
SNAKE	fire	Jan 23, 1917–Feb 10, 1918	Ting Szu	fire
HORSE	fire	Feb 11, 1918–Jan 31, 1919	Mou Wu	earth
SHEEP	earth	Feb 1, 1919–Feb 19, 1920	Chi Wei	earth
MONKEY	metal	Feb 20, 1920–Feb 7, 1921	Ken Shen	metal
ROOSTER	metal	Feb 8, 1921–Feb 27, 1922	Sin Yu	metal
DOG	earth	Feb 28, 1922–Feb 15, 1923	Zen Szu	water
BOAR	water	Feb 16, 1923–Feb 4, 1924	Kway Hai	water
(start of sixty-year cycle)*				
RAT	water	Feb 5, 1924–Jan 23, 1925	Chia Tzu	wood
OX	earth	Jan 24, 1925–Feb 12, 1926	Yi Chou	wood
TIGER	wood	Feb 13, 1926–Feb 1, 1927	Ping Yin	fire
RABBIT	wood	Feb 2, 1927–Jan 22, 1928	Ting Mao	fire
DRAGON	earth	Jan 23, 1928–Feb 9, 1929	Mou Ch'en	earth
SNAKE	fire	Feb 10, 1929–Jan 29, 1930	Chi Szu	earth
HORSE	fire	Jan 30, 1930–Feb 16, 1931	Ken Wu	metal
SHEEP	earth	Feb 17, 1931–Feb 5, 1932	Sin Wei	metal
MONKEY	metal	Feb 6, 1932–Jan 25, 1933	Zen Shen	water
ROOSTER	metal	Jan 26, 1933–Feb 13, 1934	Kway Yu	water
DOG	earth	Feb 14, 1934–Feb 3, 1935	Chia Hsu	wood
BOAR	water	Feb 4, 1935–Jan 23, 1936	Yi Hai	wood
RAT	water	Jan 24, 1936–Feb 10, 1937	Ping Tzu	fire
OX	earth	Feb 11, 1937–Jan 30, 1938	Ting Chou	fire
TIGER	wood	Jan 31, 1938–Feb 18, 1939	Mou Yin	earth
RABBIT	wood	Feb 19, 1939–Feb 7, 1940	Chi Mao	earth

Animal	Earthly branches	Calendar dates	Year name	Heavenly stem
DRAGON	earth	Feb 8, 1940–Jan 26, 1941	Ken Ch'en	metal
SNAKE	fire	Jan 27, 1941–Feb 14, 1942	Sin Szu	metal
HORSE	fire	Feb 15, 1942–Feb 4, 1943	Zen Wu	water
SHEEP	earth	Feb 5, 1943–Jan 24, 1944	Kway Wei	water
MONKEY	metal	Jan 25, 1944–Feb 12, 1945	Chia Shen	wood
ROOSTER	metal	Feb 13, 1945–Feb 1, 1946	Yi Yu	wood
DOG	earth	Feb 2, 1946–Jan 21, 1947	Ping Hsu	fire
BOAR	water	Jan 22, 1947–Feb 9, 1948	Ting Hai	fire
RAT	water	Feb 10, 1948–Jan 28, 1949	Mou Tzu	earth
OX	earth	Jan 29 1949–Feb 16, 1950	Chi Chou	earth
TIGER	wood	Feb 17, 1950–Feb 5, 1951	Ken Yin	metal
RABBIT	wood	Feb 6, 1951–Jan 26, 1952	Sin Mao	metal
DRAGON	earth	Jan 27, 1952–Feb 13, 1953	Zen Ch'en	water
SNAKE	fire	Feb 14, 1953–Feb 2, 1954	Kway Szu	water
HORSE	fire	Feb 3, 1954–Jan 23, 1955	Chia Wu	wood
SHEEP	earth	Jan 24, 1955–Feb 11 1956	Yi Wei	wood
MONKEY	metal	Feb 12, 1956–Jan 30 1957	Ping Shen	fire
ROOSTER	metal	Jan 31, 1957–Feb 17, 1958	Ting Yu	fire
DOG	earth	Feb 18, 1958–Feb 7, 1959	Mou Hsu	earth
BOAR	water	Feb 8, 1959–Jan 27, 1960	Chi Hai	earth
RAT	water	Jan 28, 1960–Feb 14, 1961	Ken Tzu	metal
OX	earth	Feb 15, 1961–Feb 4, 1962	Sin Chou	metal
TIGER	wood	Feb 5, 1962–Jan 24, 1963	Zen Yin	water
RABBIT	wood	Jan 25, 1963–Feb 12, 1964	Kway Mao	water
DRAGON	earth	Feb 13, 1964–Feb 1, 1965	Chia/Ch'en	wood
SNAKE	fire	Feb 2, 1965–Jan 20, 1966	Yi Szu	wood
HORSE	fire	Jan 21, 1966–Feb 8, 1967	Ping Wu	fire
SHEEP	earth	Feb 9, 1967–Jan 29, 1968	Ting Wei	fire
MONKEY	metal	Jan 30, 1968–Feb 16, 1969	Mou Shen	earth
ROOSTER	metal	Feb 17, 1969–Feb 5, 1970	Chi Yu	earth
DOG	earth	Feb 6, 1970–Jan 26, 1971	Ken Hsu	metal
BOAR	water	Jan 27, 1971–Feb 14, 1972	Sin Hai	metal

Animal	Earthly branches	Calendar dates	Year name	Heavenly stem
RAT	water	Feb 15, 1972–Feb 2, 1973	Zen Tzu	water
OX	earth	Feb 3, 1973–Jan 22, 1974	Kway Chou	water
TIGER	wood	Jan 23, 1974–Feb 10, 1975	Chia Yin	wood
RABBIT	wood	Feb 11, 1975–Jan 30, 1976	Yi Mao	wood
DRAGON	earth	Jan 31, 1976–Feb 17, 1977	Ping Ch'en	fire
SNAKE	fire	Feb 18, 1977–Feb 6, 1978	Ting Szu	fire
HORSE	fire	Feb 7, 1978–Jan 27, 1979	Mou Wu	earth
SHEEP	earth	Jan 28, 1979–Feb 15, 1980	Chi Wei	earth
MONKEY	metal	Feb 16, 1980–Feb 4, 1981	Ken Shen	metal
ROOSTER	metal	Feb 5, 1981–Jan 24, 1982	Sin Yu	metal
DOG	earth	Jan 25, 1982–Feb 12, 1983	Zen Hsu	water
BOAR	water	Feb 13, 1983–Feb 1, 1984	Kway Hai	water
RAT	water	Feb 2, 1984–Feb 19, 1985	Chia Tzu	wood
OX	earth	Feb 20, 1985–Feb 8, 1986	Yi Chou	wood
TIGER	wood	Feb 9, 1986–Jan 28, 1987	Ping Yin	fire
RABBIT	wood	Jan 29, 1987–Feb 16, 1988	Ting Mao	fire
DRAGON	earth	Feb 17, 1988–Feb 5, 1989	Mou Ch'en	earth
SNAKE	fire	Feb 6, 1989–Jan 26, 1990	Chi Szu	earth
HORSE	fire	Jan 27, 1990–Feb 14, 1991	Ken Wu	metal
SHEEP	earth	Feb 15, 1991–Feb 3, 1992	Sin Wei	metal
MONKEY	metal	Feb 4, 1992–Jan 22, 1993	Zen Shen	water
ROOSTER	metal	Jan 23, 1993–Feb 9, 1994	Kway Yu	water
DOG	earth	Feb 10, 1994–Jan 30, 1995	Chia Hsu	wood
BOAR	water	Jan 31, 1995–Feb 18, 1996	Yi Hai	wood
RAT	water	Feb 19, 1996–Feb 6, 1997	Ping Tzu	fire
OX	earth	Feb 7, 1997–Jan 27, 1998	Ting Chou	fire
TIGER	wood	Jan 28, 1998–Feb 15, 1999	Mou Yin	earth
RABBIT	wood	Feb 16, 1999–Feb 4, 2000	Chi Mao	earth
DRAGON	earth	Feb 5, 2000–Jan 23, 2001	Ken Ch'en	metal
SNAKE	fire	Jan 24, 2001–Feb 11, 2002	Sin Szu	metal
HORSE	fire	Feb 12, 2002–Jan 31, 2003	Zen Wu	water
SHEEP	earth	Feb 1, 2003–Jan 21, 2004	Kway Wei	water
MONKEY	metal	Jan 22, 2004–Feb 8, 2005	Ken Ch'en	wood
ROOSTER	metal	Feb 9, 2005–Jan 28, 2006	Sin Szu	wood
DOG	earth	Jan 29, 2006–Feb 17, 2007	Zen Wu	fire
BOAR	water	Feb 18, 2007–Feb 6, 2008	Kway Wei	fire

DELVING DEEPER: THE SEASONAL TABLES

*I*f you wish, you can go deeper into the analysis by examining and comparing the months of your birth as well. What is required is merely to determine in which season a person was born and then to analyze the suitability of the match from there. To do this analysis, first determine the heavenly stem element of your year of birth. Next, determine whether you were born in a summer, autumn, winter, or spring month. You will then be able to see from the chart below whether you are a strong or a weak representation of your element.

The earth element has been excluded, since earth is regarded as being equally strong or weak throughout the year, and this part of the analysis does not, therefore, apply to those born in earth years.

This chart gives an indication of the seasonal strength of the different elements. For example, if you are a wood person (that is, the heavenly stem element of your year of birth is wood) and you were born during the autumn months when it is cold and when plants usually wither, then it can be said that you are a very weak wood. If, however, you had some fire to warm you and bring you some sunlight, you would start to grow strong and thrive!

If you were investigating relationship compatibility, then you can see that for someone like you (a wood person), a fire person (someone born in a year when the heavenly stem element is fire) would be wonderful, since that person would make you strong, look after you

SEASON	METAL	WOOD	WATER	FIRE
SPRING	dying	thrives/strong	weakening	born
SUMMER	born	in bloom	dies	thrives/strong
AUTUMN	thrives/strong	dying/weak	born	weakening
WINTER	weakening	born	thrives/strong	dying

and nurture you. In this case, the elements would be exceedingly compatible and would work in your favor! Meanwhile, you would also be good for a fire person, since wood produces fire in the cycle of element relationships. In the same way, when doing feng shui, you can see instantly that a warm, red color scheme would benefit you.

Let us take another example: if you are a fire person born in a summer month like, for example, June, then you can be regarded as a strong fire person. You do not need more fire, nor do you need more wood to feed your fire. But a water person might be good for you, since the water will temper your fire and ensure that it does not grow too strong. A water person could also benefit from you, since fire will transform the water into steam, which represents energy and power. You would thus find a water person compatible. Note that, because you are a strong fire person, the water cannot destroy you.

THE HOUR TABLES

RAT HOUR
11 p.m. to 1 a.m.

OX HOUR
1 a.m. to 3 a.m.

TIGER HOUR
3 a.m. to 5 a.m.

RABBIT HOUR
5 a.m. to 7 a.m.

DRAGON HOUR
7 a.m. to 9 a.m.

SNAKE HOUR
9 a.m. to 11 a.m.

HORSE HOUR
11 a.m. to 1 p.m.

SHEEP HOUR
1 p.m. to 3 p.m.

MONKEY HOUR
3 p.m. to 5 p.m.

ROOSTER HOUR
5 p.m. to 7 p.m.

DOG HOUR
7 p.m. to 9 p.m.

BOAR HOUR
9 p.m. to 11 p.m.

EXAMINING THE HOUR TABLES

*A*nother analysis to undertake is to determine your hour of birth, since this provides additional clues to your character and personality. Chinese astrology divides a twenty-four-hour day into twelve two-hour time slots and assigns each of the animals to these time slots. Depending, therefore, on whether you are born in the hour of the Rat or Boar (or any of the other animals), some of the characteristics of these animals will overlap onto your personality reading. Make a note of the animal represented by your hour of birth, then read the relevant interpretation in a good Chinese horoscope book.

Another perspective is to use the hour to detect nuances of personal characteristics. Thus, the night-time Rat is more curious, brave, and alert than its daytime sibling. The Ox, which sleeps at night and toils during daylight hours, similarly demonstrates this trait. The Tiger hunts and prowls in the dark, and the night-time Tiger is, therefore, more dangerous and ferocious than its daytime counterpart.

The Rabbit is most alert when born in the early hours of the morning. The Dragon is also believed to come into his own during the morning, while the Snake slithers most effectively into your heart and boudoir during the early evening.

The Horse is a daytime animal, while the Sheep is believed to think best during the early evening hours. The Monkey is at its most cunning during the afternoon. The Rooster reigns supreme when born in the early hours of dawn, when his singing sounds the wake-up bell and calls successfully for the sun. The Dog's faithfulness shines forth during the night, while the Boar just goes to sleep at night.

USING ASTROLOGY FOR COMPATIBILITY

Basic personality traits are categorized initially according to the earthly branch (that is, the ruling animal) of the year of birth. Thus, if you are born in a year when the ruling branch is Tzu, you are deemed to have been born in a Rat year and will exhibit the general characteristics that rule the Rat personality. However, in any sixty-year cycle, the Rat year appears five times, each time with a different heavenly stem. So you can be a wood Rat, a fire Rat, an earth Rat, a metal Rat, or a water Rat. The attributes, temperaments and personalities of these five different rats will differ. The same is true for all twelve animals.

When investigating compatibility, it is necessary first to investigate affinity solely according to the earthly branch. This is to obtain a generalized first impression. Later you can extend this to analyses of both the heavenly stem and the earthly branch. To do this successfully, you need only read the sections on the twelve animals and investigate the two characters that make up the name of the year. With the addition of the heavenly stem, the all-important element analysis will have been added to the compatibility readings. Here compatibility is taken to mean whether the person in question will be good for you in the long run, and not whether your temperaments are suited. For attunement of temperaments, the earthly branch characteristics are sufficient to use.

To investigate the longer-term prospects of potential future partners, it is usually recommended that the season and the time of birth are also examined (see the relevant tables and information on p. 45–47 and on p. 49.)

Note that the characters on stems and branches that apply to the day of birth are not included – this is because it is impossible to present here all of the individual day combinations for the days of the past one hundred years! However, their exclusion should not affect the main part of your astrological analysis, which is based on the characteristics denoted by the year of birth.

PUTTING THINGS TOGETHER

● Once you understand how the heavenly stems and earthly branches translate into elements, you can draw up good compatibility readings for yourself and others. You can also investigate the way your ruling elements interact with those of people around you.

Contemplate the complex relationships of the Five Elements, as knowledge of the way the elements interact, according to their relationship cycles, provides much of the explanation in destiny analysis. Remember that, although destiny, as such, cannot be changed, it can be vastly improved. The Chinese believe in tien, ti, and ren – heaven, earth, and mankind luck. While you cannot control heaven luck, your earth and mankind luck lie in your hands.

Purple star astrology: fortune from imaginary stars

Purple star astrology, or Tzi Wei Dou Shu in Chinese is probably the most popular system of astrology used by the Chinese of Taiwan, Hong Kong, and South-East Asia.

"In the year of the fire horse, beware the fair maiden whose smiles entice you, and whose false sweetness hides a bitter pill, which, once tasted will hold you captive forever. Hers is a broomstick life, for she sweeps away your precious good fortune. She will make you shed a million sad tears."

*T*his divination technique is based upon the interpretaton of a person's Purple Star chart, which is divided into twelve areas representing twelve different aspects of life.

Skilled practitioners of this system are believed to be able to describe the essence of a person's character and potential. This system of fortune-telling is said to be so accurate that it can pinpoint with devastating accuracy the years and months when major changes will take place in a person's life. It can predict the hei sees or happiness occasions (marriages and births) that will come to pass and simultaneously warn you about potential conflict situations. These can refer to specific bad events happening or affect one's relationships with friends, relatives, and colleagues.

HEAVEN MEN AND DEVIL MEN
Purple Star Astrology is especially good for warning against serious misfortunes shown in the chart, thereby allowing one time to counteract or prepare for such misfortune. An excellent dimension of this method describes the "heaven men" and the "devil men" who enter one's life, with one bringing happiness and the other tragedy.

The Chinese believe that some people are good and helpful for you, while others bring nothing but problems. The secret of a happy life is simply knowing how to tell the difference between heaven men and devil men. The presence of such men is said to be clearly shown in one's life chart in Purple Star Astrology.

"Devil men" are people who will harm you, while "heaven men" are those who will be especially helpful in your life. When a skilled astrologer has given you descriptions and clues, you will have no problem spotting the good and bad people in your life. Usually, descriptions spell out the gender, age, size and height of the person so that you have no difficulty identifying them. Sometimes Purple Star can even pinpoint with amazing accuracy the month and year when you meet people whose effect and impact on your life is significant. This helps you to be on your guard.

The Marriage Palace refers to your relationship luck, and tells you if you are going to have a happy marriage, or maybe several. The stars describe what the marriage and your future spouse will be like.

It is believed that Purple Star Astrology or Tzi Wei Dou Shu, was written down and recorded during the reign of the Tang Emperors, many of whom ruled on the basis of advice given by Court astrologers. The rise to full acceptance of astrology during the period of Tang reached its peak during the long reign of the infamous Empress Wu. It is said that her astrologers successfully kept her alert to the plots and intrigues that surrounded her and that they were instrumental in ensuring her survival despite repeated assassination attempts on her life.

Purple Star Astrology was popularized beyond the Imperial palace during the Sung Dynasty. Today, rising interest in Chinese fortune-telling methods and feng shui has created a massive revival of interest in Purple Star Astrology. As a result, excellent practitioners are no longer hard to find, and life readings are now affordable. In recent years, exponents of the method have written some good software packages which can be bought off the Internet. These can be used by anyone to cast their own life chart.

THE TWELVE PALACES OF THE PURPLE ASTROLOGY CHART

1 *The life palace*
Your Fate

In a reading, the Life Palace is considered to be the most important palace because it serves as an indicator of the overall shape of your present and future life. This palace concerns itself with the general direction, characteristics, and fate of a person. It reveals inborn capabilities, predicts generalized success levels of achievement in career and in relationships, and also a person's general character. It also reveals the potential for development, along with wealth-earning capabilities.

2. *The brothers and sisters palace*
Your Siblings

The Brothers and Sisters Palace indicates the number of siblings you have and the quality of your relationship with them. This palace also serves to define your relationships with those outside the immediate family – with business partners, colleagues, and friends who work closely with you.

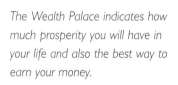

3 *The marriage palace*
Your Relationship Luck

The Marriage Palace indicates whether or not you will enjoy a happy marriage. It shows the possibility of multiple marriages and indicates when marriage luck is missing. This is what causes some people to be single all their life. The stars in this Palace describe the characteristics and quality of the marriage, and of the spouse, and in some cases can even describe the kind of person your spouse will be and whether your marriage to this person will be successful and happy.

4 *The children's palace*
Your Children Luck

The Children's Palace indicates your children luck. The stars can accurately indicate the number of children in a family. It reveals the nature of your relationship with your children, and some experts also interpret this palace as referring also to employees and personal students.

5 *The wealth palace*
Your Future Fortunes

The Wealth Palace shows the extent of, or lack of, wealth in your life. It shows how hard you have to work to achieve a good income and it can foretell the periods when you will become a millionaire (if ever!). Those destined to have gambling luck or windfall fortune luck can also be revealed. This palace accurately describes your financial situation in general. It indicates the best way for you to make your money, your wealth luck periods, and your earning capacity.

The Wealth Palace indicates how much prosperity you will have in your life and also the best way to earn your money.

Opposite: The Brothers and Sisters Palace shows the number of siblings that you have and your relationship with them.

6 *The health palace*
Your Well-being

The Health Palace is like a barometer of your physical wellbeing. Good astrologers can pinpoint with remarkable accuracy when you might face the danger of serious illnesses or accidents, and even indicate periods when fatal conditions prevail. It can also indicate what type of sickness you are particularly prone to. This is an important palace of which to take note.

7 The travel palace
Your Hometowns

The Travel Palace reveals the places where you will stay during your lifetime, whether stuck in your hometown or halfway across the world. It defines which options bring what kind of career luck. It describes all of your relationships and explains whether you are lucky in one place or whether it is better to move to another town.

8 The friends palace
Loyalty and Betrayal

The Friends Palace describes the luck you have with friends. Loyalty and betrayal are the two ends of the friendship yardstick and these are emphatically revealed in the chart. Bad stars indicate a life of betrayal by people close to you. Good stars show that you always have lots of "heaven" men in your life. You can determine whether your business partners are good or bad from the stars located here.

The Parents' Palace describes your relationship with your parents and with bosses at work. It can also show inheritance prospects.

9 The career palace
Your Power Prospects

The Career Palace offers predictions on the development of your career, and whether you will become successful as a career employee or as an entrepreneur, being your own boss. This palace's stars will indicate the kind of career you should pursue and the sort of achievement you can expect.

10 The property palace
Your Territories

The Property Palace is an indicator of wealth. If the stars here are good, it indicates an amassment of real estate through your life, while bad stars indicate blockages to the ownership of property. This palace also reveals the quality of your living environment.

11 The fortune palace
Your Inner Self

The Fortune Palace reveals your thinking process and behavior. It describes whether you are a positive or negative person and specifies the length of your life. This palace either strengthens or weakens the readings made from the Life Palace, and sometimes positive changes to life conditions can be made if this palace is blessed with good stars. The Fortune Palace reveals hidden tendencies in you toward spiritual growth and meditative practices.

12 *The parents' palace*
Your Elders

The Parents' Palace focuses on your relationship with your parents and with bosses in general. It indicates the prospect of inheritance, and it can reveal whether your parents are separated or divorced.

THE IMPORTANCE OF INTERPRETATION

Tzi Wei Dou Shu incorporates time analysis in the readings, and these can be classified into periods of ten years, or as annual periods. It is a very sophisticated calculation which has the capability to map out the luck cycle broken down to every hour, if required. Fortune-tellers usually undertake Purple Star readings in conjunction with Four Pillars. The findings of both systems generally complement each other, even though the methods and the basis of analyses are different.

The purple stars have "yang" energy. Each of the thirty-six stars has the strength and ability to influence the mind and action of people. Each star can bring luck or misfortune, although their effects depend on people's reaction to what is predicted. Predictions should be viewed as warning signs. The unfolding of your life depends on your responses to the events brought by your heaven luck.

So, although Purple Star Astrology is an accurate system of fortune-telling, the outcome of your life and decisions should never be regarded as being carved in stone. It is best viewed as a guidance manual for living and preparing for the future.

The life chart differentiates between the heaven, earth, and mankind charts and, depending on which is stronger, you will get a feeling for the sort of person you are – either fatalistic, or action-oriented to change your destiny. Those with bad and ruinous stars should look out for the transformation stars, as these can change misfortune stars into good luck stars. How your life turns out depends upon the brightness of the major and minor stars in the relevant palaces. When wealth stars are bright, money is indicated; when relationship stars are bright, this means there is heaven men luck. And when power stars are bright, life will be blessed with achievements.

The Chinese almanac:
the book of days

There are those who claim that *The Chinese almanac* was created 4,000 years ago. Since then the Chinese people have treated it with reverence, regarding it as a divine and spiritual guide to living. Today people still consult the almanac before undertaking any important activity.

SPECIAL EVENTS

The Chinese consider that the following events should only be undertaken during auspicious days and times; otherwise, the potential for success and for things going smoothly is severely limited.

● Moving into a new house.
● Moving into a new office.
● Starting a new business.
● Starting a new job.
● Launching a new product.
● Signing an important contract.
● Starting renovation work.
● Opening a new branch office.
● Starting construction work on a new project,
● Embarking on an important journey.
● Getting married.
● Celebrating important birthdays.
● Sowing new seeds for the new season.
● Starting the harvesting.

*I*t was in Hong Kong, where I went in 1982 to take up an appointment as the new CEO of Grindlays Dao Heng Bank, that I came to understand the widespread belief in the *Almanac* and the important role played by it. Published as an annual *The Book of Days*, it was – and remains – the bestselling book there. During the time of the Emperors, however, not just anyone could publish the Almanac, for it was issued only under the Imperial seal. In fact, it is this association with the Emperor that has led to it becoming regarded as a divine and spiritual guide to life.

During my Hong Kong days, I discovered that each time we planned the opening of a new branch, launched a new product or issued a new financial instrument, my managers always recommended days that had been selected on the basis of the *Almanac's* advice concerning auspicious days. My local Chinese staff considered the almanac to be an indispensable tool for doing business. Indeed, every right-thinking Chinese businessman considered the selection of an auspicious day as a key factor in the successful outcome of any business venture.

In recent years, the popularity of *The Chinese Almanac* has spread beyond the shores of Hong Kong, enjoying a parallel revival of interest alongside feng shui. This *Book of Days* offers annually updated and detailed advice for each day of the calendar year, and there are many Chinese who take the *Almanac* so seriously that they will never make major decisions regarding timing without consulting it.

Generally, however, different masters use different calendars for calculating the days identified as good and bad in the *Almanac*. There are some who base their calculation on the lunar calendar, and there are other masters who prefer using the Hsia, or solar, calendar. In addition, different experts use different formulas for working out good and bad days: some use the daily Lo Shu (or magic square) ruling numbers, while others use the Five Elements to undertake their analysis.

I would advise that you consult only those Chinese almanacs that have been authored by reputable and experienced masters of the calendars. As for the almanacs that have been translated into English, there are, of course, some excellent translations around, but, once again, my advice is to consult only those that have been calculated by reliable masters.

The Chinese Almanac covers every day in the year and is highly respected by the Chinese people, who use it to find auspicious days for major or new ventures. Good translations are available, but always choose one that has been calculated by a respected master.

The easiest way to select auspicious days is to consult the *Almanac*. Many people also believe that the *Almanac* is a powerful book, which has the ability to protect a household from mischievous spirits. This belief springs from the many different Taoist talismans and amulets reproduced in the *Almanac*. Some masters even recommend that you place the book in the vicinity of the main front door, as an antidote for any harmful chi that may inadvertently enter your home. Certainly, when secret poison arrows threaten the home, the mere presence of this book is believed to nullify their effects.

If you happen to chance upon a comprehensive Chinese version of the *Almanac*, it is a good idea to flick though its pages and look at some of these talismans. You might then wish to reproduce these powerful deflectors of potential misfortune and keep them near at hand to ward off bad luck.

To understand the system of days in the *Almanac*, it is useful to know that each month consists of two periods of fifteen days each. These continue from year to year and are referred to as the "joints" of the year. The periods correspond to the days when the sun enters the first and fifteenth degrees of each horoscope sign.

Your destiny in your hands:
chinese palmistry

The Chinese believe that the extremities of the human body reflect the profile of a person's mind, body, and spirit. Thus, the outer appearance of hands, feet, and head – the five extremities – offer clues to the inner consciousness and destiny of any individual. Lines and indentations on the hands therefore reveal a great deal, as do those on the feet. And massaging the hands or the feet can often give relief to a multitude of body aches and pains.

Your hands communicate with your mind, body, and spirit all the time, so that their appearance, shape, and lines, as well as the signs and tell-tale markings on the palm, offer remarkably accurate clues to your fortunes and misfortunes. Over time, the Chinese have developed guidelines and principles for analyzing the lines of the palm and the appearance of the hands in order to assess their impact on life destiny.

A HAND IN THE FUTURE

There are fundamental indications on the hands that are said to be so "obvious" in indicating good or bad fortune and character that these "rules" have been passed on from grandmother to mother to daughter. As a result, many of us who are of Chinese origin (even those living outside China) are aware of them.

For example, we know that a thick, firm palm indicates a good life, while a bony, limp palm is an indication of a life perpetually short of both money and good health. Palms with clear lines are said to be preferred to those where the lines are feathery, broken, or light. When there are too many lines on the palm, they indicate a confused mind, lacking direction and purpose.

Gaps between the fingers, when they are held close together, are considered a sign of an inability to save and to amass wealth. This is usually the case when fingers are knobbly. If you look carefully at your own hand and those of other people, you will notice that rich people usually have fingers that fit very snugly next to each other, so that no "holes" show through.

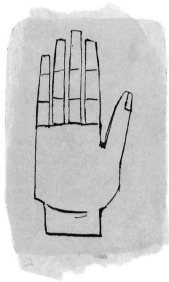

square palms: METAL

slender palms: WOOD

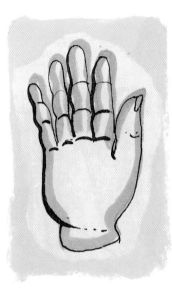

fleshy palms: WATER

elongated palms: FIRE

heavy palms: EARTH

WHICH IS YOUR HAND ELEMENT?

● Square palms with matching fingers belong to the metal element.

● Slender palms with long, elegant fingers belong to the wood element.

● Round, fleshy palms with round fingers belong to the water element.

● Elongated palms with pointed fingers belong to the fire element.

● Thick, heavy palms with similar fingers belong to the earth element.

As with face-reading, feng shui and other astrological practices, the principles that underlie hand analysis are related to the categorization of hands according to the Five Elements. Thus, all hands are classified according to the elements of wood, fire, water, metal, and earth, and the element of your hands should, ideally, "match" the element of your year of birth (this refers to the "heavenly stem" element). You can check your year element by referring to the lunar tables shown on pp.45–47. Armed with this element, you can check it against the category to which your hand belongs and from there determine whether

KEY

I *Squares = protection*

2 *Vertical crosses = obstacles*

3 *Crosses = severe problems*

4 *Islands = unhappy periods*

5 *Circles = obstacles*

6 *Tridents = huge career success*

7 *Stars = big success*

8 *Wavy lines = ups and downs*

9 *Upward lines = many opportunities*

10 *Solid, clear lines = a strong, decisive person*

your hand "matches" your personality, based on your year of birth. The way to determine the kind of hand element that is best for you is to follow these two guidelines:

1 A hand element that repeats your year element is good.

2 A hand element that "produces" your year element is even better. So, a water-element hand is great for a wood-year person; a wood-element hand is great for a fire-year person; a fire-element hand is excellent for an earth-year person; an earth-element hand is great for a metal-year person; and a metal-element hand is good for a water-year person. These conclusions are based on the reproductive cycle of the Five Elements. In the same way, you should also watch out for hands whose element clashes with (destroys) the year element. Earth destroys water, which destroys fire, which destroys metal, which destroys wood, which destroys earth.

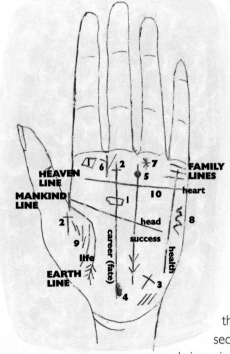

THE LINES OF THE PALM

● The three principal lines on your palm - the heart, head, and life lines - are regarded as heaven, mankind, and earth lines, as shown in the diagram.

● When these main lines are deep, clear, and have no interruptions, this is a sure sign of a successful, smooth life. All secondary lines branching off these main lines are good when they run upwards and bad when they run downwards.

● In addition, there are three vertical lines on the palm. The first and innermost is referred to as the Jade Pillar, and governs career luck and fortune at work. It is generally known as the fate line. If this line is long and ends with an auspicious marking, such as a star or trident, the indication is that you will have fabulous fortune. The second vertical line is referred to as the Six Elegances, and brings six successes, namely wealth, good name, family happiness, high rank, good descendants, and high spiritual attainments. This line is also known as the sun line, but not everyone has it on their palms. Those who do and whose line is long and uninterrupted by circles or islands, and ends in a star, square, or trident, will enjoy all six types of success. The third and outermost vertical line is the health line, whose appearance on the palm indicates ill health.

THE GOVERNING TRIGRAMS

The Pa Kua

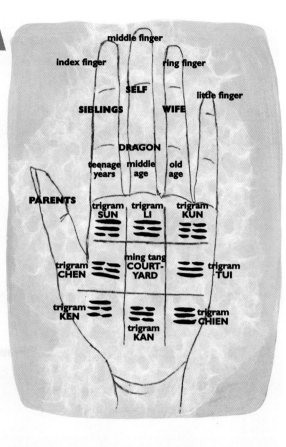

Lines and markings on the palm are also studied according to the Later Heaven arrangement of the eight trigrams of the Pa Kua. For this purpose, the eight-sided symbol of the Pa Kua is superimposed onto the palm of the hand. Thus, in addition to providing confirmation of other "signs" on the hand, markings also offer clues concerning good and bad luck in different dimensions of your life. This is indicated by the governing trigram in the different parts of the hand.

If you study the hand shown here, look first at the way the different parts of the palm have been segmented. In the center is the courtyard, or ming tang, which is similar to the life palace of the face (see p. 70). When this part of the palm appears weak or shows a deathly blue or black color, it is a sure sign of impending accident or even death. The center of the palm should always look bright and healthy, like a prosperous valley surrounded by hills created by the mounts of the outside eight trigrams. If it is indented or shows a bony appearance, then the life indicated is full of difficulties and sorrow.

● The trigrams Sun, Li, and Kun are the happiness trigrams, and positive markings in any of these areas indicate great good fortune. In Sun, stars, tridents, and upward-moving lines mean prosperity and that your wealth luck is strong. Squares mean that your assets and wealth are protected. Negative markings here indicate loss of wealth and income. So a cross or an island indicates money problems.

● In Li, positive markings mean that you will enjoy great fame and that your name will be honored and highly respected. Negative markings suggest the opposite.

● In Kun, positive markings mean that you will enjoy a happy marriage and family life. Stars and tridents in this part of the hand indicate that you will marry into wealth. For women, having a positive marking here is an especially auspicious indication.

SIGNS TO LOOK OUT FOR

● When the courtyard, or ming tang, looks bright and healthy, it indicates a life of happy events. There is plenty of good descendants luck and a man will be blessed with a good wife. The courtyard should be deep but not bony.

● When all eight trigrams show well-formed "mounts" (that is, when you can discern the appearance of raised flesh in these eight areas of the palm), it is a sure sign of high office and prosperity. You will have plenty of servants.

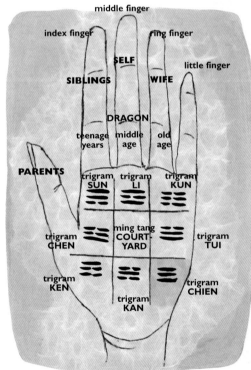

A pronounced mount in the area of the Chien trigram means five generations' worth of good fortune.

● When the place of the trigram Chien has a pronounced mount, it means that you will head a family whose fortunes will be good for at least five generations. This reading is particularly good for men, since Chien refers to what is paternal. It also means that you will benefit enormously from friends and benefactors, whose patronage will make you rich and powerful.

● When the mount in the Kan trigram is pronounced, it indicates that your family will be of great help to you and that you can enjoy tremendous good fortune in your work, as it will be recognized. Positive markings here, such as the "fish" sign, are especially auspicious and mean that your life will get better and better as you grow older.

● The trigram Ken refers to your relationship with siblings and your earlier life. When this mount is well pronounced, it suggests a very good start in life. Whether or not this early promise can be fulfilled will depend on the other markings on your palm.

THE MEANING OF THE FINGERS

● Flat fingers indicate a life of hard work.

● Round fingers show intelligence.

● Fingers with bony joints are a sign of laziness - there will be little success for such people.

● Stiff fingers with hard nails indicate courage.

● Soft fingernails mean a short lifespan.

● Fingers of the same length and height indicate little chance of success.

● The thumb tells you about your parents. An upright thumb is most auspicious and beneficial.

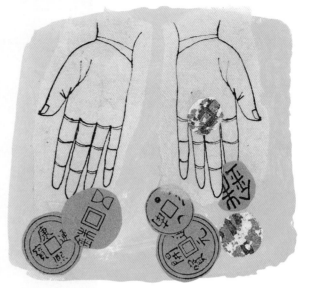

● The index finger governs power. When it is long and elegant, it indicates influence and a long life; when it is short and fat, it suggests money but little influence. When it is damaged, it indicates a serious illness.

The middle finger of the hand is known as the Dragon. The Dragon is energized when this finger is the longest and when it is also longer than the palm, which brings good fortune.

● The middle finger is the Dragon. For there to be good fortune, this finger should be the longest. When that is the case and when this finger is longer than the palm, the Dragon is said to be energized and there is good luck. When it is short and overshadowed by the palm (signifying the White Tiger), then luck tends to be mediocre.

● The ring finger should always be the shortest of the three central fingers; otherwise, there is a tendency towards vanity and weakness – friendships are likely to be short-lived and marriages unhappy. In the old days, women with long ring fingers often found it difficult to find husbands, as families would reject such women as bringing bad luck to their spouses.

● The little finger relates to old age. A long little finger shows that old age is happy and abundant; a crooked little finger indicates sadness.

Looks and luck: Chinese face-reading

"His face is square, balanced, bright, vigorous. He has a high and noble forehead. This man is destined to hold power. Her face is smooth, round, resembling an egg. Her cheeks are plump and smooth, eyes bright as moonlight on a cloudless night... She will be much cherished during her lifetime."

The Chinese have always believed that heads and faces impart the true essence of a person's character and that the general directions of someone's destiny can be revealed as much through face-reading as through astrological reading based on dates of birth.

Chinese face-reading reflects the influence of the fundamental underpinnings of Chinese wisdom, so that, as in other sciences, the quality of face energy or chi is analyzed on the basis of physical and structural balance, symmetry of features, apparent firmness and the quality of yang chi. The Pa Kua of Later Heaven arrangement is superimposed onto the face in order to ascertain the quality of the respective trigrams. These trigrams are represented by parts of the facial features, and what they reveal – good or bad – depends on what each part of the face shows. Generally, an auspicious head is round or square with a high forehead.

For men, a full, round head that neither protrudes nor has indents, moles, or black spots indicates long life, wealth, and nobility of name. Heads that are perfectly round are especially auspicious, and such a man is also said to be honorable and upright.

There is a popular saying among the Chinese: "A square face favors men, and a slightly elongated round face [oval] favors women." When a head is square, the forehead should be high. It should look neither too oily nor excessively dry. This indicates that a man has the makings of a "king" or maybe a head of state.

One of the most auspicious faces for a man is thought to be a square-shaped one with a high forehead (opposite). For a woman, however, an oval face with a high forehead is preferred.

In modern times, successful tycoons, CEOs, and all sorts of leaders can be defined as "kings." If you look at pictures of international business and political leaders, you will note that the most successful, most admired, and most prominent are generally those who have at least two out of three of these features: they have a round or square head that is well-balanced, a high forehead, and a clear, bright complexion.

When the forehead is slightly protruding and fleshy, this is a sign of high office. When the forehead looks parched or stretched, with the bones showing through thin skin, it is a sign of loneliness and even poverty. Some master face-readers suggest that this is an indication of a very bad ending, when wealth and assets and all your family will be lost. At its worst, it indicates premature death. Thus, thin facial skin is bad, while thicker skin covering the forehead is a sign of longevity. When the bones seem to protrude prominently, this suggests an early life of hardship and suffering; when the head is sharp or pointed, high office is impossible to achieve.

For both genders, a big head with small shoulders suggests a life devoid of family – there is little descendants' luck and marriage destiny tends to be stale and unhappy. When there is a small neck as well, this suggests premature death.

For women, a perfectly round head is a sign that she will have good children, who will look after her in her old age. She will enjoy a life of leisure with few worries. Women with round heads and good complexions, whose faces also have plenty of flesh, usually bring good luck to their husbands. Pointed heads bring bad luck, and when the jaw is wide and protruding (however slight the protuberance), such a woman brings unhappiness, tragedy, and even death to her spouse.

UNDERLYING FACIAL COLOR AND MOLES

Faces should have the color of yang chi, which is indicated by an inner glow. Such faces, that have an underlying tinge of healthy red, indicate wealth and prosperity. This is usually confirmed by the color of the palms, which should also be very red – fleshy, deeply red-colored palms are one of the surest indications of a life of wealth. When the face is very fair, underlying bones that look pale white indicate poverty. A purplish tinge is glorious, while a bluish coloring suggests nobility.

It is better when there are no veins on the face, since these are suggestive of problems. Veins that look green or blue may indicate dishonest intentions, so you should be a little cautious about anyone with many of them.

Moles on any part of the face are not generally a good sign and if you have any (or if your face is covered with several "black spots"), it is a good idea to have them surgically removed. Black moles on the face, especially if they are exposed, are usually a sign of premature death. Red moles on the face, on the other hand, are said to be excellent indications of good fortune. They should be small and be a light brownish-red color. Located near the mouth, they suggest plenty to eat and are a sign of excellent oratory skills. Similar moles near the eye area attract the goodwill and friendship of powerful mentors. High above the forehead, red moles indicate affluence and power. On either side of the ear, they suggest high spiritual attainments, especially when the ear lobes are also long.

Moles of any size or color found in the center of the face suggest a life marred by lost opportunities and accidents. If possible, try to have them surgically removed, especially if they are found between the eyebrows on the Life Palace.

Moles on the chin and neck areas are said to bring career success. All hidden moles on the front of the body are good, while all moles on the back of the body indicate a life filled with burdens and problems.

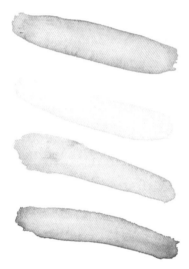

For good wealth, the Chinese believe that your skin should have some healthy tones of red. If it is very pale in color it is thought to indicate some poverty.

Dry, flaky skin, like fading, brittle leaves, is thought to indicate bad luck.

CHARACTERISTICS OF THE FACE

A long face that is narrow and looks like a Modigliani painting is an indication of hardship, work, and toil. Such a facial shape could also indicate one great failure during middle age. When the texture of the face is horizontal, it suggests disharmony. If you meet someone like this, it is better to avoid him in the future.

When the face is protruding at the top and bottom and looks like a crescent moon, with the forehead and chin jutting out and the middle portion indented, this suggests a scheming disposition. This may not necessarily be bad, but such a person tends also to be gossipy and political, so avoid getting too chummy with someone like this.

When the flesh of a man's face is bubbly and loose, and appears to "shake" when he is running or dancing, it indicates that harm will come to the wife and children. When the face has an orange-peel-like skin, characteristic of cellulite, a life of loneliness is possible. On the other hand, when the face appears "oily," some loss of wealth may occur. A powdery face is said to attract the chi of lechery and wantonness; a dry, brittle face has no luck.

Facial skin should be vital and healthy like fresh leaves and have the appearance of yang chi with an underlying red glow.

These indications are especially useful for modern-day women, who can easily do something to improve the texture and shape of their faces with the clever use of make-up. Go for the look that makes your face shine with luminosity and light. Yang energy brings good fortune, so the face should always appear "alive" and happy. Always put on a smile, and do not hesitate to use eye make-up and bright lipsticks to jazz up the yang energy of your face. If you suffer from sunken cheekbones and a hollow look, increase your food intake and use blusher to bring colour back to your face. Always choose clear, pure colours, and strive to achieve a certain luminosity. This will greatly improve the feng shui of your face.

A popular Chinese ditty goes something like this: "A man's face depends on its vigor. A woman's face depends on its color."

Generally, a white face on the surface indicates a frightened, shy nature. If you want to become more self-confident, consider using darker foundation and some color on your cheeks. Use a pink or purplish tinge to attract the chi of an easy life filled with happy occasions, and an olive, yellowish tinge to create good earth luck.

If your face is excessively red, use a good foundation to reduce the suggestion of this fiery color. Faces that are too red on the surface are excessively yang and could attract disaster, so scale down on the color. It is never a good idea to use blue- or green-based or -tinged powder. This will give an "evil and treacherous" appearance and will attract all sorts of unsuitable people into your life.

THE PALACES OF THE FACE

Detailed readings of the face can be analyzed by studying the different "palaces" of the face. These palaces govern different kinds of luck and are shown in the illustration opposite.

There are two areas of the face that indicate a life of wealth and prosperity: the forehead and the nose. When the top of the forehead or the nose, or both, are well endowed with firm flesh, this is a sure sign of a life of wealth. Good foreheads also indicate success in public life and a sound reputation, while a big, fleshy nose simply means plenty of money — in fact, the bigger and rounder the nose is, the greater the wealth luck. On the other hand, when the forehead is bony and the nose is small, little wealth luck is indicated.

Your children luck (that is, the number of children you have — sons or daughters — and how filial they will be) is indicated by the appearance of the face just under the eyes. Generally if you have a slight "fold" here, it indicates good descendants luck — you will have dutiful children. When this part of the face (the palace of the children) has a pinched look, indicates a lack of descendants luck. Dark circles under the eyes are

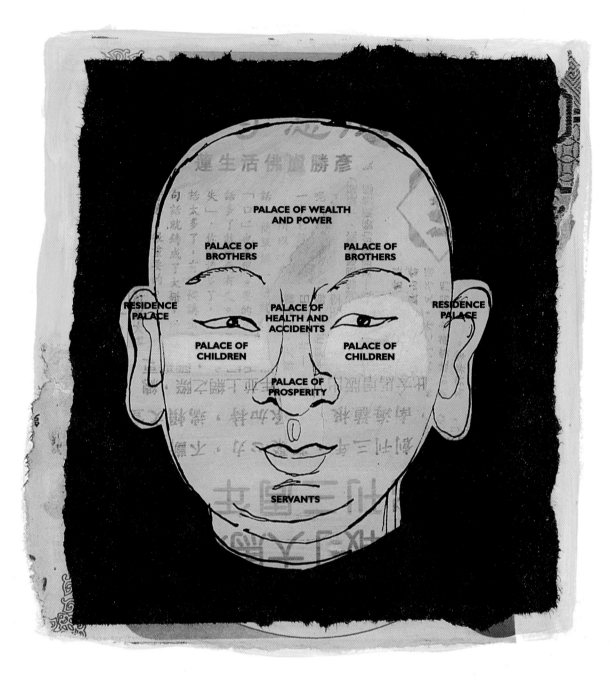

PALACE OF WEALTH
AND POWER

PALACE OF
BROTHERS

PALACE OF
BROTHERS

RESIDENCE
PALACE

PALACE OF
HEALTH AND
ACCIDENTS

RESIDENCE
PALACE

PALACE OF
CHILDREN

PALACE OF
CHILDREN

PALACE OF
PROSPERITY

SERVANTS

usually not a good sign, so you should always make sure that you get enough sleep; if dark circles persist, use a camouflage stick to improve their appearance. This will also improve your children luck.

Siblings luck (that is, how well you get along with your siblings) is indicated in the area above the eyebrows. When this part of your face has an indentation, it means that your siblings will depend on you and sometimes even cause you grief. If the flesh is firm and smooth, however, your brothers and sisters will be of enormous support to you.

For a detailed reading, the "palaces" of the face, which relate to different types of luck, are studied in detail. A fleshy nose, for example, indicates good wealth.

FACIAL STUDY

● Study your face carefully and take note of the color and thickness of your skin in the different areas. Note the locations and color of moles, look out for indentations, and analyze your flesh to see if it is firm or loose and whether the pores are large or smooth. Remember that discolorations, black spots, and indentations in a specific area indicate problems at a particular age, while a smooth, unblemished skin is a sign of plain sailing.

When the property and residence palaces of the face appear full and well-endowed, it means that you will live in a mansion. When they are thin-skinned and pale, you have little or no asset luck.

The most important palaces are those that are located along the central line of the face, especially the life palace. This area between the eyes should look clear, bright, and firm of flesh. Any moles, discoloring or indents in this area suggest that you will have to deal with major obstacles and mishaps. If there are any markings further down, along the bridge of the nose, they indicate accidents during middle age, when you are in your forties.

The nose governs your wealth luck, while the area under your mouth shows the number of people who serve you, either as employees or as subordinates. The more well-shaped this area is, the more likely it is that you will be a boss rather than a subordinate.

DESTINY BY AGE AS REVEALED IN THE FACE

According to Chinese folklore, a person's life moves from point to point on the face, and these respective ages are shown below.

Note that the childhood years are governed by the markings on the right and left ears. The teenage years and the early twenties are indicated by the forehead. Generally, the smoother and larger this part of the face, the greater the indication that you will sail through these years. Marks and indentations, black spots, creases, and moles here indicate obstacles, accidents, poor health and problems related to your relationship with your parents.

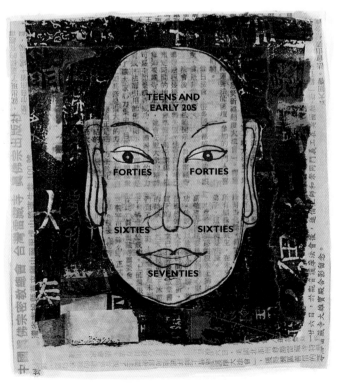

When the forehead is flawed in some way, this means that there tends to be difficulty in communicating with parents. When this part of the face is small and bony, the indications are that parents will lack the resources to give you much of an education. You will tend to be a loner and have difficulty relating to other people. On the other hand, when the forehead is broad, round, and smooth, it is an excellent indication of a happy period ahead.

The Chinese gods of wealth

The worship of spirits, deities, and special beings in Chinese tradition is often focused on obtaining some benefit of a material kind, so wealth gods abound in their pantheon of deities.

TSAI SHEN YEH

As with other deities, the Chinese Gods of Wealth are a hazy composite of many different legends and stories. One popular prosperity deity is today known as Tsai Shen Yeh, a personage often depicted sitting on a tiger and wearing elaborate dragon robes. A full-frontal dragon is emblazoned magnificently on the front of his robe. In his right hand, he carries a symbolic ingot of gold and a bundle of coins, suitably tied with yang-energy red thread. Cradled in his left arm is a staff bearing various precious symbols. His expression is fierce, but also relaxed. There are many manifestations of this popular deity – some are sitting, while others are standing. When placed in the home, his image is believed to bring the chi of wealth and prosperity.

The generally accepted tale of his origin describes him as a hero of the Chou dynasty who fought on the side of the last of the Shang emperors in the second millennium BC. He is said to have performed many wonderful feats of endurance and valor: he could ride a black tiger and hurl pearls against his enemies that exploded like firebombs. Eventually, however, he was defeated by black magic spells, which succeeded in casting him into the netherworld of spirits, where he remained captured and imprisoned until his eventual release. By then, tales of his bravery on the battlefield had reached legendary proportions. He was venerated as the head of the Ministry of Riches and Prosperity and hence came to be worshipped over the centuries as the God of Wealth.

Tsai Shen Yeh is still universally revered in China, and images of him can be seen everywhere, especially among the poorer classes. One stunning symbol often associated with him is the tree of wealth. This is a tree whose branches comprise strings of dollar notes and whose fruits are ingots of gold, which can be obtained by lightly shaking the

In Chinese symbolism, the tree of wealth carries dollar notes, gold ingots, or precious gems.

tree. Like other magical manifestations, the tree of wealth is said to have an inexhaustible supply of gold, silver, and precious stones. Today, with a jaundiced modern eye, it is tempting to view such stories as simplistic fairy tales, yet there is no denying that both the God of Wealth and the tree of wealth are still regarded as chi-laden sources of prosperity luck.

If you wish to invite Tsai Shen Yeh into your home, make sure that you have prepared a prominent place for him to sit. He should always face the front door: not necessarily directly, although, if he does do so, this is perfectly acceptable. He can be placed in a corner of the living room or foyer that is diagonal to the main door, and should always be set on a table, never on the floor.

FUK LUK SAU

Then there is the extremely popular trinity, the Deities of Wealth, Prosperity, and Longevity, known as Fuk Luk Sau. Their images are exceedingly sought-after, and only the Laughing Buddha matches their popularity in Chinese households. Fuk Luk Sau is best placed in the dining room of a house. Many families have several sets, locating them both at home and in the office of the breadwinner.

I myself have three sets of Fuk Luk Sau: one in my family dining room, one in my family television room, and one in my living room. This is because the meanings associated with these three star gods are simply so auspicious. Basically, they signify overall good luck, bringing harmony to the home and overcoming any negative vibes. They also bring good health, lots of prosperity and plenty of descendants' luck.

Sau is the God of Longevity. He is often shown wearing robes that bear the longevity symbol and carrying the nectar of immortality in his bottle gourd. Fuk is the God of Wealth and carries a *ru yi*, the symbol of authority, to signify power and success while. Luk, the God of Prosperity, carries a child to signify descendants' luck. Both Luk and Fuk wear mandarin robes that signify nobility (and hence wealth).

TUA PEH KONG

Another popular Taoist deity, who is worshipped as the Hokkien God of Wealth, is Tua Peh Kong. He is usually shown seated on a throne dressed in robes that feature the longevity symbol, indicating that the wealth he brings to households will last for a very long time. In his right hand he carries the *ru yi*, itself a most auspicious symbol. A jade *ru yi* is believed to confer fabulous luck on those who want

PLACING THE GODS

● Never put images of any of the Gods of Wealth in your bedroom, as this is said to be most inappropriate. You may set them in the dining room and living room, where it is most beneficial if they are placed in a corner that corresponds to your most auspicious direction under the KUA formula, or based on your animal year of birth. These lucky sectors are based on different methods of feng shui, details of which can be found in my feng shui books.

The most popular gods of luck to bring good chi into the home include Fuk, Luk, Sau – the Deities of Wealth, Prosperity, and Longevity (clockwise, from top left), and Tsai Shen Yeh.

power and authority. Here, the God of Wealth is shown carrying it to emphasize the great good fortune that he is able to bestow upon those who ask him for wealth and success. In his left hand he holds an ingot of gold. His expression is one of benign compassion.

OTHER GODS OF WEALTH

There are two other Gods of Wealth: military and civilian aspects of the same deity, said to be the deified image of a former sage known as Pi Kan, who lived during the twelfth century.

Another popular deity, worshipped as a powerful protective deity as well as a God of Wealth, is the canonized hero from the warring-states period of China's history. This is the God of War, Kuan Ti (Kuan Kung). He is always shown in full military regalia with a red face and a fierce countenance. Place Kuan Kung directly facing the entrance to an office or household to prevent people with negative intentions from entering.

Prophetic dreams and the
eight immortals

"I dreamed I met an old sage walking leisurely along Phoenix mountain pass. He carried a musical instrument shaped like a bamboo tube. Greeting me with a smile, he introduced himself as Kuo-Lao Chang. This Immortal held his hand out to me, and I alighted daintily upon it ... I wondered then if I were a human dreaming I was a butterfly, just as now I wonder if I am really a butterfly dreaming I am a human..."

Chief Immortal Chung-Li Chuan.

*T*he Eight Immortals are the superior beings of Taoist legend. They are said to have lived at various times, each having attained immortality under different circumstances by drinking the nectar of the peach of immortality. The Immortals are revered as symbolic of longevity and good fortune. They are shown singly or as a group of eight crossing the waters. Each Immortal is associated with a special symbol, which enables him or her to manifest supernatural powers. The eight are therefore believed to possess the secrets of Taoist magic. Their symbolic presence in homes (frequently depicted on Chinese porcelain vases and urns, on plates, in paintings, or as statues in any medium) is believed to bestow good health, happiness, and general good fortune on families. It is for this reason that they are such popular subjects among artists and craftsmen.

THE SPECIAL POWERS OF THE IMMORTALS

Each of the Eight Immortals represents a special wisdom that is helpful in coping with life's circumstances, and each of their symbols expresses a significant ability or power. If you display them singly in your home, it is useful to understand what each signifies.

1 *Chung-Li Chuan*
Immortal of Health

The chief of the Eight Immortals is Chung-Li Chuan, who has a fat, exposed belly and carries a magical fan, which he uses to cure the sick. He symbolizes good health and possesses curative powers. His presence in the home is believed to bring health and longevity.

2 Kuo-Lao Chang
The Immortal of **Wisdom**

The second Immortal is Kuo-Lao Chang, who carries a musical instrument that looks like a bamboo tube. He possesses the wisdom of the ages and has the ability to make himself invisible. This Immortal is regarded as a sage whose image bestows wisdom on the family patriarch. He is said to appear in dreams to bring good tidings or warnings of impending disaster.

3 Dong-Pin Lu
The **Immortal** of **Protection**

The third Immortal is Dong-Pin Lu, a reclusive scholar revered as the patron saint of the sick. He is said to have learned much of his magic craft from the chief of the Immortals. On his back he carries a sword, which he uses to overcome hungry ghosts and slice through suffering caused by bad chi. In his right hand is a fly whisk, which he uses to cure illnesses. His image in the home is an amulet against illness and the bad energy caused by wandering spirits.

Dong-Pin Lu, the Immortal who signifies the essence of protection.

4 Guo-Chin Tsao
The Immortal of **Patronage**

The fourth Immortal is Guo-Chiu Tsao, said to be related to an empress of the Sung dynasty. He signifies nobility and is dressed in official mandarin robes. His symbol is a pair of castanets, which he holds high up in his left hand. These symbolize his noble birth. Tsao is said to bestow recognition and to attract high office for the family patriarch. Politicians and those wishing for a life of power should invite his image into their home.

Guo-Chiu Tsao, the Immortal who symbolizes the luck of patronage.

5 Tieh-Guai Li
The **Immortal** of **Magic**

The fifth Immortal is Tieh-Guai Li, who looks like a beggar, but is reputed to be adept at supernatural magic. He bears a gourd, from which emanates nectar and all kinds of auspicious objects. On his back he carries magical headgear, which he uses to demolish people who have evil intentions.

An image of Li in the home is said to be a safeguard against "devil men" (see p. 52) — that is, people in life whose intentions and motives are suspect.

The eighth Immortal, Hsien-Ku Ho

6 Hsian-Tzu Han
The Immortal of the Natural World

The sixth Immortal is Hsian-Tzu Han, who makes sweet sounds on his flute. This attracts good-fortune chi to him, so all animals, insects, and plants thrive in his presence. Han's special ability is to make plants bloom instantly – he keeps a profusion of plants in the sack that he carries on his back. Those of you who love gardens will benefit from his image in the home.

7 Tsai-Ho Lan
The Immortal of Prosperity

The seventh Immortal is said to be a young man who goes searching for the three-legged toad. Eventually, he finds it by tempting it with golden coins tied with red and gold thread. Since then, the three-legged toad has always been associated with wealth and prosperity, and in Chinese art it is usually depicted with a coin in its mouth.

8 Hsien-Ku Ho
The Immortal of Women

The eighth Immortal is another woman, a fairy called Hsien-Ku Ho. Her emblems are the holy lotus and the fly whisk. Her presence in the home benefits the matriarch.

PROPHETIC DREAMING

The Immortals are associated with "yogic dreaming," also known as the art of inducing a state of sleep. One of them – especially the second or third of the Immortals, Kuo-Lao Chang or Dong-Pin Lu – may appear in your dreams to impart some special prophecy affecting your life. Such prophetic dreams are said to be visually rich in detail. When practised correctly, the person experiencing the dream will awaken with a vivid recollection of it; but unless the dream is properly recorded, by lunchtime all knowledge of it will have been lost. Taoists take dream-inducing, and especially the inducing of auspicious dreams, very seriously indeed.

One method passed on to me by a Taoist master in Hong Kong many years ago uses the techniques of visualization and concentrated mental focusing prior to going to bed. You need to concentrate on one of the Immortals – any one of them with whom you feel an

"If you need a prophecy relating to some problem or decision that needs to be made, you can ask for a dream that shows you the most beneficial way to proceed."

affinity. Or you can pick one from among the three star gods, Fuk Luk Sau – the Gods of Wealth, Prosperity, and Longevity (see p. 74). A statue of Lao Tzu, the sixth-century BC founder of Taoism, also makes a good object for concentration. All these Taoist personalities are featured prominently in Chinese art, so it is not difficult to obtain their image.

Place this near the head of your bed, behind the headboard. The image should be higher than the bed, so that when you sleep the figure of the Immortal or Taoist deity is directly behind your head. Just before you go to sleep, invoke the aid of the superior being by lighting an incense stick, bowing reverently and politely requesting that you have a prophetic dream. If you need a prophecy relating to some problem or decision that needs to be made, you can ask for a dream that shows you the most beneficial way to proceed.

Next, lie down on your right side, with your right palm upwards between your face and the pillow. Try to get to sleep as quickly as possible, but if you cannot, then just before you doze into slumber repeat your request again. Remember to place pen and paper within easy reach, so that should you awaken in the middle of the night, with the dream still vivid in your memory, you can jot it down and then go back to sleep again. If you do not do so, you will forget the dream by morning. Record your dream as accurately as possible, but leave the analysis for later.

Taoists believe that any dream remembered with great coherence and clarity has a hidden message, and indeed that is so. Three years ago, I dreamed vividly of two white tigers. I remembered the dream clearly, and the image of the white tigers (or what I thought to be tigers) has stayed in my mind to this day. Shortly afterwards, I had the good fortune to meet a Tibetan high lama, Lama Zopa Rinpoche. Meeting Rinpoche completely changed my life (for the better), but it was much later – after I discovered the stunning beauty of Tibetan thangka paintings – that I recognized the snow lions usually painted on the thrones where Buddha sits as the white tigers of my dream!

Buddhists also believe that prophetic dreams which reveal important spiritual messages can generally be induced by chanting special mantras and then sleeping with fresh kushi grass under your pillow and mattress. This long grass is normally used to make brooms, and you can obtain some by pulling strands of it from a new broom.

Kuo-Lao Chang, the Immortal of Wisdom, is believed to assist one to obtain prophetic dreams.

A FUTURE MESSAGE?

● Chinese spiritual practitioners are strong believers in rituals such as prophetic dreaming. I have to confess that over the years I have discovered that, whether or not I believe in the supernatural beings of Taoism, there is definitely something mysterious in the results of my investigations into induced prophetic dreaming. My advice is to adopt the attitude that initial failures need not be taken to mean that success is impossible. You could very well be pleasantly surprised when you least expect it.

Buddhism and the six
realms of existence

The Chinese believe strongly in an afterlife, and in many lives beyond this life. Chinese folklore is filled with colorful stories of wondrous paradises that comprise the ten states of heaven. Equally vivid are the horrific descriptions of hell — frightening places of eternal torture and suffering.

"Heaven and hell are surely nothing more than states of mind and so are well within our control, if only we know it."

I remember being taken as a child to the Har Paw gardens of Singapore, where images of hell had been put together in one frightening tableau after another. That visit left a powerful imprint on my young mind, so that to this day I can recall vivid images of heaven and hell as was portrayed in that Asian equivalent of Disneyland.

Having now been exposed to the Buddhist influences on Chinese beliefs and culture, I realize that those re-enactments of heaven and hell in Har Par gardens must have reflected the Buddhist belief in six different types of rebirth or existence, three of which are in the dreaded "lower realms" of existence.

The first three are the lower realms and Buddhists pray throughout their lives never to be reborn into these realms. Such rebirths are believed to be the manifestation of ultimate bad karma. It is negative karma that propels one into the lower realms.

1 *The hell realm*
Place of Fire and Brimstone

The hell realm is a place of extreme cold and extreme heat, physical torture and a state of continuous hunger and thirst. Those whose list of misdeeds causes them to fall into hell may end up staying there for thousands of eons. It is this belief that prompts Buddhists — and especially high Buddhist teachers and practitioners — to spend their lives saying prayers for those in the hell realm. This is the compassionate manifestation of their religious practice.

2 The realm of the hungry ghosts
Place of Starvation and Thirst

In the realm of the hungry ghosts, inhabitants simply lose the karma to eat or drink, so there is massive starvation and thirst. It is only when special prayers are dedicated to them that they may partake of small drops of water to quench the fire in their throats.

Anyone who falls into the realm of the hungry ghosts has to stay there for a thousand years, until the prayers dedicated to them are powerful enough to release them. It is for this reason that those who are highly accomplished in their spiritual practices through meditation are never afraid or in awe of these wandering hungry spirits. On the contrary, those who have the wisdom to realize the extreme suffering of hungry ghosts feel nothing but compassion for them. In Buddhism, many advanced practices undertaken by high lamas and holy monks are directly dedicated to rescuing these wretched souls.

3 The animal realm
The Result of Anger or Generosity

Often, the cause of rebirth in this realm is due to specific negative karma. However, some animals, such as pets, can enjoy relatively good karma in that they live pampered lives. We also hear of dogs or cats who have been left enormous fortunes by their owners; they have the karma of wealth, but not the karma to control their wealth.

4 The human realm
Place of Conscious Life

This is the most fortunate realm to be born into. When you realize that here is where you can exercise control over an intelligent mind, you will begin to understand how precious human rebirth is.

5 & 6 The paradise realms
Gods and Demi-Gods

The two pleasure realms, or the form realm and formless realm, are where those with enough good karma get reborn. These realms are also known as the deva realm, where Gods and Goddesses live in a state of coninuous abundance. These are not places of bliss or the best places for rebirth, since here one soon uses up all of one's good karma and, having exhausted it, all pleasure beings normally sink to the lower realms, to restart the cycle of birth and rebirth.

APPRECIATING HUMAN LIFE

● Much of Buddhism centers around gaining the experiential insight to realize just how precious this life of ours is. In the teachings, many metaphors have been used to demonstrate the great rarity of human rebirth. Indeed, when I am told that I could have once been a worm, an ant, or a fish, I realize that, although the world population constitutes a very high figure, it is truly nothing compared to the trillions and trillions of "living beings" that abound in the universe.

● A perfect human rebirth implies having the karma to be born into places where there is no war, famine, disease, or pestilence. It is said that being born as a human amid fierce fighting and conflict, into war zones and countries of perpetual drought and poor harvest, is like being born into hell. And yet, because the human mind is a powerful conscious life form, this is the best rebirth.

● When you realize the preciousness of life, you will understand that the genuine good fortune in everyone's life arises from nothing more than one's very existence as a human being.

The three manifestations of
karma

Every action produces an effect. The cause always precedes the outcome, or the effect. So karma is the law of cause and effect, and man, because of his actions, is the master of his own destiny.

*K*arma explains why each person is unique, in physical appearance as well as in mental disposition. It explains the inequities and tragedies of Creation: the sadness of the child born into extreme poverty; the slaughter of innocents; famine, war, and painful death – surely these cannot be adequately or easily accommodated in the notion of an all-compassionate Creator God?

The law of cause and effect is both a reasonable and a logical explanation for the tragedy of Creation itself. Accepting the explanation of karma suggests that we, and not God, are in control of our destiny. We have to accept that we are responsible for the situations in our lives. This is because karmic law affects everyone in equal measure.

HOW IS KARMA CREATED?

It is taught that all actions, speech, and thoughts combine and continue indefinitely from one rebirth to another, with no underlying substance to make them permanent. This is the wheel of life and it persists indefinitely until the cause for its continuation becomes extinguished through the perfection of wisdom, which encompasses compassion; or, to put it another way, until enlightenment is attained.

Karma is like a form of chi energy. It has no beginning, but it has an end. Buddhists speak of beginningless time and of enlightenment, when karma ends. There are Three Manifestations of karma and thus three types of karmic effects of your bad and good deeds.
There is karma created in this life:

● Whose results are effective in this life
● Whose results are effective in the next life
● Whose results are experienced after many lifetimes.

Karma that is repeated becomes very powerful. Karma that is practised in relation to a powerful object, such as your parents or spiritual guru, also becomes powerful. This is true even of the smallest act of harm or disrespect, or of service and respect. Thus, taking care of your aged parents creates good karma.

Acts of devotion and respect that are practised in relation to the guru, to Buddha, *dharma* (meaning the ideal truth) and *sangha* (venerable monks and nuns) are also highly beneficial, as these are also powerful objects. Consequently, you can experience in this life the suffering results of negative actions committed against the guru, Buddha, *dharma,* or *sangha*, as well as the favorable results arising from any small virtuous actions that you have carried out in relation to these personages.

It is believed that to reach enlightenment (nirvana) we must stop going around in circles and instead seek wisdom.

KARMA KNOW-HOW

Karma and rebirth explain:
● That the sufferings we encounter are all of our own doing
● The inequalities of mankind: why some are born "better" than others
● The birth of the world's geniuses, such as Einstein and Mozart
● The different destinies of siblings, although they come from similar backgrounds
● Spontaneous negative passions, such as greed, anger, and jealousy
● The feeling of like and dislike on first sight
● The good and bad in us from past lives
● The sudden transformations of good into bad, and vice versa
● Changes in fortunes, accidents, and premature deaths
● The birth and rebirth of highly realized holy men, precious gurus, and lamas, who are perfect spiritual teachers with incomparable physical, mental, and intellectual powers. These "living Buddhas" return to earth again and again to lead us towards liberation from the cycle of rebirth to enlightenment. They are termed Bodhisattvas, or saints.

THE FOUR PRINCIPLES OF KARMA

1 Karma is definite

This means that, having committed an action, you will definitely experience the appropriate result according to the kind of action done: virtuous action brings positive results, while non-virtuous action brings suffering results.

2 Karma is expandable

This means that once karma is created, its results will be experienced in many, many future lifetimes. Thus the suffering result of a non-virtuous action will be experienced repeatedly, not only in this life but in hundreds – or even thousands – of lifetimes to come. So you should not be careless, even in doing one small negative action, in the mistaken belief that "This won't hurt me." It is mentioned by Buddha that one small fire spark can burn piles of hay that are mountains high. Likewise, you should not assume that one small virtuous act will not benefit you: by collecting drops of water, you can fill a large bucket! Therefore, in practising remembrance and awareness, it is a good idea to abandon even the smallest negative action and to practise even the smallest virtue.

3 Karma always has a cause

If you haven't created the karma – that is, if you have not done the action that is its cause – you can never experience the result.

4 Karma created is never lost

This means that, once karma has been created, it will not disappear of its own accord. If virtuous or non-virtuous karma is not interrupted, then it will never get lost. However, if karma is interrupted, then it can be destroyed.

For example, by purifying a non-virtuous action, you can interrupt the potential to experience the suffering result. In order to interrupt negative karma, you must purify it through practices such as making a strong confession. If you have created negative karma, such as the ten non-virtues or other negative actions, then living your life feeling

CHANGING KARMA

In the Buddhist teachings on the path to enlightenment, six methods are given to purify karma.

1 Reading the profound sutra texts.

2 Meditating on emptiness.

3 Reciting special powerful mantras.

4 Making holy objects, such as statues, stupas, and paintings.

5 Making offerings to your spiritual guru or master.

6 Reciting the names of the powerful Buddhas.

There are thus six methods that you can use to purify negative karma. I have been taught the practice of the Buddha of Purification, Vajrasattva. This is an extremely potent method of purification, which can easily be incorporated into your daily life.

scared, upset, and depressed is not the solution. The solution is to do something immediately in order to purify the negative karma. When negative karma is created, it must be purified before you die. This is most important

PURIFICATION PRACTICES

If you commit one small negative action today – for example, killing a tiny insect – and do not purify that negative action by the end of the day using Vajrasattva practice, then the results of that action will multiply day by day. After eighteen days, the negative karma created will have become 131,072 times heavier, and, as each month and year goes by, that one tiny karmic action eventually becomes the size of this earth.

In Buddhism, negative action, such as killing a small insect, needs to be cleansed daily to stop it from accumulating. One purification method is to do Vajrasattva practice, which involves saying its four-syllable mantra at least twenty-eight times a day.

By doing Vajrasattva practice (see p. 87) – even by reciting the 100-syllable mantra at least twenty-one times, or the four-syllable mantra at least twenty-eight times – negative karma is stopped from increasing day by day, month by month and year by year. Not only does reciting this mantra purify today's negative karma, but it also purifies the negative karma of past lives.

When you perform the Vajrasattva mantra and practice, and you also meditate upon the four opponent remedial measures – the admission of wrongdoing, the feeling of regret, the deep resolve not to repeat the wrong action, and the taking of refuge with the Buddha – you create a perfect and powerful purification practice.

THE KARMA PURIFICATION PRACTICES

Karma is another way of explaining heaven luck. Karma means that the quality and condition of your present life is determined by you and by your own actions in this life and in previous lives. Your life condition is not determined by an almighty being – it is the result of your own actions, words, and thoughts. Bad and good karma are determined by the good or bad that you do, speak, and think.

The reality of life is that all human beings repeatedly commit what are termed by Buddhists non-virtuous actions. For instance, the non-virtue of killing includes the smallest act of killing any life form. So when you unthinkingly slap a mosquito to death, or when you go fishing or hunting and succeed in catching your prey, that is killing. As long as the intention to "kill" is there, you will have incurred some negative karma.

Buddhist monks and nuns who take the vow not to kill are extremely mindful, even when they walk, that they do not inadvertently step on an ant. This might sound extreme to the layperson, but it was explained to me that this is part of a Buddhist's mind training and transformation. I was told that it is this kind of intense mindfulness that leads to the successful practice (eventually) of pure morality. Buddhists are also mindful that:

● Negative actions, no matter how small, multiply the moment they are committed, unless they are purified immediately. Even the smallest non-virtuous action can, therefore, transform itself into super-large negative karma. Hence one needs to be ever-mindful.

● Ignorance is not an accepted excuse for performing a non-virtuous action. Although it is possible to commit a non-virtuous action without realizing you have done so, the negative karma is still incurred!

Practising Buddhists, therefore, always assume that we are continually committing negative karma, which needs to be "purified" on a daily basis. This is one of the most compelling reasons for offering prayers. At every prayer session, some form of confession thus takes place. This is not unlike the Catholic confession, or the prayers of forgiveness of many mainstream Western religions, which draw the attention of the mind to some form of daily or weekly accountability of thoughts, words, and deeds. This represents living in a state of "mindfulness."

"To go from darkness to darkness is bad continuing to be bad. From light to darkness is good becoming bad. From darkness to light is bad becoming good. From light to light is good becoming even better. These are karmic causes and effects."

In Buddhist teachings, there are many methods of purifying karma. These are usually worked into the daily routines of monks and nuns, who spend their lives in monasteries and include practices such as reading profound sutra texts and meditating on them; contemplating the state of Emptiness; reciting powerful mantras daily; making holy objects such as statues, stupas, or paintings of Buddhas or the holy scriptures; making offerings to their spiritual guru, or teachers, whom Buddhists regard as actual living Buddhas; and reciting the holy and powerful names of the different Buddhas. These methods of purifying karma make up many of the daily meditation rituals of Mahayana Buddhism.

One interesting attitude of the Chinese is the widespread belief that religious and spiritual practices can be "delegated" to monks, who will undertake to chant prayers on their behalf, thereby helping in the purification process. Since negative karma is believed to create blocks to success or victory, arranging for such prayers to be said on their behalf is a popular practice among many Chinese families. Indeed, this is something that is done at least once a year during the new year period, or whenever a member of a family gets seriously ill.

THE 100-SYLLABLE MANTRA

VAJRASATTVA PRACTICE

This is the practice of reciting a 100-syllable mantra twenty-one times each night as part of the four remedial opponent measures of taking refuge with the Buddhas, generating great regret at having committed a negative action, reciting the mantra, and making a solemn promise to yourself not to repeat the negative action.

Most followers of Chinese and Tibetan Buddhism receive oral transmission of the mantras from their spiritual teachers, so they usually know this 100-syllable mantra. There is also a short version, the four-syllable mantra OM VAJRASATTVA HUM, which can be chanted twenty-eight times as a substitute practice until you meet a qualified lama or abbot who can transmit the 100-syllable mantra to you. As I am not qualified to do so, I cannot reproduce the full mantra here.

Not only does reciting this mantra purify today's negative karma, it also purifies the negative karma of your past lives. And, by performing the Vajrasattva mantra and practice in conjunction with meditating on the four remedial opponent measures, it becomes a perfect and powerful purification practice.

Kuan Yin,
the buddhist madonna

Many Chinese believe that just by thinking of Kuan Yin's image and calling her name, their burdens grow lighter, their worries are allayed, and their wounded hearts heal. The compassion of the Goddess of Mercy has the power to cause the fire of looming disasters to cease burning instantly; the power to transform enemies into benefactors; to loosen bonds that imprison; to dissolve all evil intentions; to dispel all spells; to chase away all fierce beasts and cause snakes to lose their poison.

"A Buddhist madonna who protects and saves, rescues and liberates, Kuan Yin is a Bodhisattva who answers every prayer."

Kuan Yin is China's Buddhist madonna. She personifies – even more so than Lord Buddha – the practice of Buddhism among the Chinese. There are few Buddhist households in Asia that do not have an image of the goddess Kuan Yin, for she is the divine being who is turned to most often in times of grief and sorrow. Everyone benefits equally from the benevolence of this great goddess.

There are thousands of stories that speak of her swift, compassionate answer to prayers. In history books and story books, in religious texts and academic treatises, all research ever undertaken on this Buddha highlights the one quality – compassion – that is synonymous with her name.

ORIGINS

Chinese theologians who have undertaken painstaking research into the origins of this popular deity explain Kuan Yin as the female manifestation of the Buddha of Compassion, Avalokiteshvara, of Indian origin. Legends abound concerning the many manifestations of this beloved goddess, who is said to manifest herself to beings in forms to which they are able to relate. Some date the transformation of Kuan Yin from male to female to the fifth century, during the time of the North-South dynasties of China. Others contend that the feminine form appeared only from the eleventh century. Since it is the essence of this goddess that is significant, however, the timing of her historical appearance does not seem important. But understanding the widespread popularity of Kuan Yin does offer stunning insights into the Chinese psyche.

The most popular tale of Kuan Yin's origin relates that she was the beloved princess Miao Shan, whose purity at first angered her father, the king. Despite many obstacles and his fierce opposition, she eventually succeeded in convincing her father to take the virtuous path towards enlightenment.

This she did by cutting her own arms and sacrificing her eyes to cure him of his illness. The legend of Miao Shan presents Kuan Yin as the beautiful, all-forgiving, all-compassionate princess. Dressed in white robes, she is always depicted with a serene expression on her face. Kuan Yin is, of course, the Buddha of Compassion, Avalokiteshvara,

Kuan Yin is considered by the Chinese to be the goddess of compassion. She is normally depicted looking serene in flowing white robes, sitting on a lotus or standing on a dragon or tortoise, holding a bottle of nectar in one hand and a fly whisk in the other.

who has assumed different forms throughout the centuries. Some say that she may even have taken reincarnation as Queen Maya, who gave birth to the Lord Buddha Shakyamuni and passed away seven days later. According to other sacred texts, the Buddha of Compassion has even manifested himself as a bull to convert a butcher; and in Japan, Kuan Yin (or Canon as she is known there) is believed to have reincarnated once as their sacred goddess Amaterasu Omikami. To Tibetans, His Holiness the Dalai Lama himself is a manifestation of the Buddha of Compassion. Whatever manifestation she has taken, however, the essence of the compassionate goddess Kuan Yin remains the same.

Kuan Yin represents hope for the hopeless, and herein lies her timeless appeal. Throughout the years, I have heard many wonderful tales of the way she has answered the prayers of my mother, and of my mother's friends. In recent times, since discovering Buddhism for myself, I have seen at first hand how Kuan Yin has touched and transformed so many lives, including my own, with her divine blessings.

REPRESENTATIONS OF KUAN YIN

I love Kuan Yin in all of her "thirty-three manifestations and fourteen bestowals of fearlessness." These different images of her provide a wealth of inspiration for those who wish to practice her meditations.

Kuan Yin as princess Miao Shan is the most popular, as she has a most benevolent expression on her face. Kuan Yin is also depicted as a four-armed goddess, and this is believed to be the form to visualize when you need to pray for courage or when you are engaged in litigation and require her help with conflicts and contentious situations.

Finally, there is the image of the 1,000-armed Kuan Yin, who also has sixteen heads. Each arm ends in a hand with an all-seeing eye, so that Kuan Yin in this form sees all, illuminates all, and helps all. The 1,000-armed Kuan Yin embodies the union of compassion and wisdom that leads to enlightenment.

Kuan Yin is the embodiment of the Bodhisattva in all of us. Bodhisattva is a Buddhist term meaning a divine being who has attained perfection and whose only wish and purpose are to help all other beings. The nearest equivalent in Western tradition would be an angel – a benevolent angel – someone who watches over you, invisible and powerful, someone ever-ready to hear and respond to your heartfelt call for help.

"She is the light of the blind, the shade for those who suffer from the heat, the stream of water for the thirsty, and the bestower of fearlessness for those who abide in fear. She is the remedy for those who are ill and a mother for all suffering beings."

PRAYER TO THE 1,000-ARMED KUAN YIN

Here is a simple and enchanting sadhana to the 1,000-armed Kuan Yin, which incorporates the chanting of the famous Kuan Yin mantra.

1 Visualize

In the space in front of you, visualize the divine form of the 1,000-armed Kuan Yin. She stands on a beautiful lotus and white moon seat. From her body shines forth radiant white light. She is youthful-looking and her garments are decorated with magnificent jewels.

2 Think

I go for refuge until I am enlightened in the Buddha, the dharma, and the sangha. With the merit I create by practising compassion and other perfections, may I attain Buddhahood for the sake of all beings.

3 Then say from the heart

"O Arya, Compassionate-Eyed One, you are the treasure of compassion. I request you: please listen to me, please guide me, mothers and fathers, in all the six realms of existence, to be freed quickly from the great ocean of samsara. I request that the vast and profound peerless awakening mind may grow within me. With the tear of your great compassion, please cleanse all negative karmas and delusion. Please lead, with your hand of compassion, me and all mother migrators, to fields of bliss. Please, Buddha Amitabha and Kuan Yin, Compassionate Buddha. In all my lives be my virtuous friends. Show me the pure path that leads to enlightenment, and quickly place me in Buddha's state."

4 Recite

OM MANI PEH MEH HONE, the famous six-syllable mantra of the Buddha of Compassion, while doing the meditation and the visualization.

Kuan Yin is sometimes depicted as having 1,000-arms and sixteen heads. Each arm has an all-seeing eye so that she can see, illuminate, and help everyone. She is thought of as the embodiment of compassion and wisdom that can lead people to enlightenment.

After each verse, visualize white light coming from Kuan Yin, flowing into your body and completely filling you. This practice purifies the selfishness, the self-cherishing mind, the ignorance, the attachment, and the anger that prevent you from understanding the real meaning of life. The white light blesses you and enables you to under-stand and integrate kindness and compassion into your life. If you wish to, you could meditate on the Eight Verses of Thought Transformation (see p. 152).

The amulets and talismans of
taoist magic

Belief in a supernatural realm is so deeply embedded in the Chinese psyche that the application of metaphysical cures via talismans and amulets is both widespread and popular.

This Taoist amulet illustrates the celestial Kings of the Four Directions. Talismans, such as this one, were thought to be able to destroy negative energy brought about by wandering spirits.

*I*n addition to bringing good luck, amulets are believed to offer protection against spirits and black magic. Belief in a spirit world, and in the existence of powerful practitioners of "negative magic," is widespread in all the countries of Asia and throughout China. This has made the use of protective talismans an important dimension of life among the Chinese.

Many different types of materials are used in amulets, to ward off negative vibrations that are believed to bring accidents, illness, robbery, and physical discomfort. In the old days, the use of Taoist amulets was widespread, and many of the antique almanacs feature different kinds of talismans.

Although a variety of materials was used in the fashioning of these talismans, rice paper that was colored yellow or green was always extremely popular. On these pieces of paper would be written special characters, deemed to have the power to keep bad luck at bay. Illustrated here (see left) is an example of a Taoist amulet drawn with the celestial Kings of the Four Directions. These talismans were credited with the power of dissolving negative energy caused by wandering bad spirits. Different characters could be written for different purposes. Thus there were special protection amulets for pregnant women to protect the unborn child from coming to any harm; and for protection against accidents, fire, water, and so on.

Handwritten amulets were believed to be especially powerful for warding off physical harm, and gave protection from armed assault and robberies. There are Taoist masters who are particularly adept at writing these protective amulets. They draw special characters on rice paper after chanting some Taoist prayers. I have carried protective amulets for over twenty years and have found them to be really potent in warding off physical danger. I have also seen them work for others in rather dramatic circumstances.

AMULETS FROM THE CHINESE ALMANAC

The Chinese Almanac, or *Tung Shu* (see also p. 58) contains some of the more common amulets that continue to be used these days. You may wish to copy some of these charms onto yellow or green rice paper.

The charm shown here (right) is a general house-protection amulet, which guards against negative influences caused by people with bad intentions toward you. It is also believed to offer good protection against robbery. You can copy it onto yellow or dark-green paper and then paste it directly above your front door, outside the house and facing outwards. This amulet is also believed to be effective against spells being cast on members of your household.

There are also charms written on paper that are effective at curing high fevers and other ailments. According to the Chinese almanac, you should copy such a charm onto a piece of yellow rice paper, burn it, and then place the ashes in water and drink the water. This will bring the fever down quickly.

The yellow charm shown here is very effective against any bad chi or negative spirits that you feel may be haunting your house. All you have to do is copy it and attach it to the part of the house where you sense strange vibrations.

The charm on the beige background (above) is thought to be effective for eye ailments and abdominal pains. Traditionally, the charm is burned, the ashes are put in water, then the water is used to bathe the eyes. If the sufferer has abdominal pains, the water is drunk.

This is a general house-talisman for protecting your house against robbery and other bad intentions.

Left: This charm is effective against any bad chi or bad spirits you feel may be haunting your house. Copy and fix the charm to the part of the house where you sense strange vibrations.

The charm on the near left is for eye ailments and abdominal pains.

Feng shui and
earth magic

Feng shui is the ancient Chinese practice of living in a state of balance with the physical environment in order to benefit from the surrounding energy and enjoy good fortune. In the many manifestations of its potency, feng shui is akin to Chinese earth magic.

Feng shui has been practised for more than 3,000 years. In recent times, this ancient practice has experienced a world-wide resurgence of interest – a renewal akin to a renaissance of all the techniques that have been developed over the centuries concerning how to live in balance with the earth's forces. The practice of feng shui directly addresses the quality of the surrounding energies that permeate the atmosphere, and feng shui masters derive their knowledge and wisdom from the landscapes of the environment.

These ancient masters analyze the interactive effects of orientations to discover correlations between the mysterious metaphysical energies of the earth and man's fortunes. They study how living with positive energy brings good fortune, while living with negative energy causes illness, accidents, and misfortune.

Such masters have gained impetus in their investigations from the very air that we inhabit – invisible, yet powerful, throughout the living spaces that make up our environment. They refer to these invisible, intangible forces as chi or, more colorfully, the "celestial dragon's cosmic breath." When this breath is benevolent, it brings auspicious good fortune to all who breathe it; when it is destructive, it causes misfortunes to befall all who come into contact with it. The masters term this negative energy the "killing breath."

When homes are located, orientated, or arranged in a way that taps into a huge amount of benevolent chi, then this cosmic breath will bring good fortune. A home that is bathed in good chi benefits every member of the family, and particularly the patriarch. In addition, when the home is correctly surrounded by the four symbolic celestial animals – the dragon, the tiger, the tortoise, and the phoenix – then this great good fortune is perpetuated from descendant to descendant for at least five generations.

ANCIENT ORIGINS

For many hundreds of years, feng shui was practised by the ruling classes of Imperial China. From the Tang dynasty right up to the last of the Ching rulers, feng shui remained an important part of Imperial Court practice and feng shui masters were often revered for their knowledge. Sometimes, however, they were executed to ensure that others would not use their mastery against the Son of Heaven. In an atmosphere of continuous Court intrigue, emperors protected their feng shui secrets with cunning and care.

Chinese folk tales are filled with tales of feng shui's impact on the birth and death of dynasties. The founder of the Ming dynasty in 1368, for instance, who was a beggar and a bandit, was believed to have succeeded in overthrowing the last Mongol emperor to create the Ming dynasty because of the radically favorable feng shui of his father's grave.

Chinese history books describe how, upon becoming emperor, Chu Yuan Chuan ordered all feng shui masters to be put to death. In some old stories, it is even speculated that he caused fake feng shui books to be written in order to confuse the knowledge of this prac-tice. When Yong Le later became the third Ming emperor and began construction of the new northern capital (what is now the Forbidden City in Beijing), it is speculated that his architects and builders used some of these fake books to arrange the feng shui of the new palace. It was perhaps this that caused the palace to be burned down almost immediately after it had been completed.

The architectural history of China's Forbidden City is filled with speculation concerning the input of feng shui. When the Manchus overthrew the Ming dynasty in the seventeenth century, they too subscribed to feng shui. Indeed, the emperor Chien Lung took a personal interest in the subject and succeeded in introducing correct feng shui features. His reign was one of prosperity and good fortune for his people, and feng shui may well have played a major role in bringing this about. Chien Lung-period coins are highly prized as amulets of good fortune.

"Chinese history books describe how, upon becoming emperor, Chu Yuan Chuan ordered all feng shui masters to be put to death."

Even Chairman Mao Tse Tung, who openly derided the practice of feng shui, was said to have benefited from the good feng shui of his grandfather's grave. It was said to reside in the palm of the Heavenly Moon Goddess, a particularly auspicious configuration for a grandson of the family.

In the twentieth century, even the latter-day "emperors" of China – Mao Tse Tung and Deng Xiao Ping, communists who scoffed openly at feng shui – are believed to have benefited from the excellent feng shui of their ancestors' graves. Mao's grandfather's grave was said to reside in the palm of the Heavenly Moon Goddess, a configuration so auspicious that it was to bring great good fortune to the grandson of the family. In Deng's case, the feng shui fable concerns his father's grave, as well as the presence of three auspicious peaks within sight of the family home.

Feng shui did not flourish in the China of Mao Tse Tung. In fact, during his period of power, the practice of it was strictly forbidden. Mao lived his whole life obsessed by the fear of being overthrown, and he took no risk of anyone using feng shui luck to overthrow him.

THE RISE OF TAIWAN AND HONG KONG

Feng shui has now crossed the waters to other countries of the world and especially to places to which Chinese people who have fled the motherland have migrated. Today there are more than sixty million Chinese who live outside China, and many of them subscribe strongly to the influence of feng shui on their living conditions.

In fact, many feng shui masters followed the Kuomintang General Chiang Kai Shek to Taiwan, taking with them precious texts and invaluable feng shui Luo Pans, or compasses, which contained the trade secrets of many old masters. The ruling élite and entrepreneurs of Taiwan thus benefited greatly from excellent feng shui knowledge. It is no coincidence that both Taiwan and the Kuomintang flourished during the middle years of the twentieth century. Taiwan continues to be one of the richest and most successful countries in the world.

Feng shui also took root in Hong Kong, to which numerous southern refugees moved and where they built new homes. Many of the wealthier immigrants brought with them the feng shui knowledge of their forefathers and, like their counterparts in Taiwan, used feng shui to great advantage in their new homes (at the time under British colonial rule).

Today, Taiwan and Hong Kong are widely acknowledged to be economic success stories. There are many who attribute their success to the almost universal application of feng shui guidelines.

Feng shui techniques concerning spatial arrangement were applied not only in places of residence but also in offices, workplaces, factories, and commercial developments. At first, only the surrounding environments were diagnosed to ensure auspicious orientations. Building exteriors were oriented to capture the protection of hills and feed from the symbolic wealth of the waters of the harbor. Roads were built in accordance with dragon/tiger symbolism and the classical tenets were carefully followed. But, as cities grew and modern buildings mushroomed, urban living

Hong Kong is seen as one of the successes of feng shui practice. The buildings were planned so that they got the protection of the hills behind and the benefit from the good chi of the water flowing in front in the harbor.

As Hong Kong developed, feng shui practitioners studied their Lo Pan compasses to come up with answers to deal with their new modern surroundings. They looked at how to bring old compass formulas into the new environment, and worked out how to deal with obstructions that were caused by the tall buildings.

took over and feng shui guidelines began to penetrate right to the interiors of buildings and into peoples' homes. Soon, whole new interpretations of the old tenets began to surface, which were adapted to modern living conditions.

Master practitioners studied their inherited Luo Pans to try to discover answers to deal with the new surroundings. Novel interpretations of all the old symbols began to take root in the psyche of modern living. Masters also deliberated on secret compass formulas and began to incorporate them into modern environments, in the process experimenting with methods of dealing with feng shui obstacles caused by man-made buildings. Many of these formulas, which were so jealously guarded in the past, are now beginning to see the light of day.

MODERN-DAY FENG SHUI MASTERS

Many modern-day feng shui masters now have access to these valuable feng shui formulas. There is little that is secret these days, especially when so many Chinese and Taoist masters living in various parts of the world are now generously sharing their expertise. Feng shui courses flourish in many countries, as a result of which hitherto-unknown interpretations have surfaced.

Many of these interpretations call for knowledge of the basic fundamental principles of feng shui — principles that encompass the two different arrangements of trigrams around the eight-sided Pa Kua, the twenty-four mountains around the compass, the Five Elements and their different cycles, the principles that govern the balancing of yin and yang energies, the Lo Shu square, and much more. Increasingly, more and more people are becoming familiar with feng shui terminology, and as more educated people study feng shui technology in earnest, many of China's feng shui secrets are beginning to be shared with the world at large.

A few years ago, feng shui was almost unknown in the West. Today, it enjoys fast-growing mainstream appeal. This interest will continue to soar, simply because, as they learn to apply the formulas of earth magic and to live harmoniously with the environment, more people will start to benefit materially from its practice. The popularity of feng shui is sure to rise. The same potency that ensured its survival in China throughout the last few thousand years will now fuel interest in it throughout the world.

After benefiting from the richness of Chinese wisdom, it is a good idea also to tap into the secrets of the living earth. Suspend your skepticism and discover another way of looking at the energies that permeate the environment. Discover depths of meaning in the simplicity of the yin/yang cosmology. Tune into the subtleties of the Five Elements in your surroundings as they interact continuously with one another, and then apply these ancient wisdoms to the practice of some Chinese earth magic.

Feng shui is not difficult to learn or practice. The hard part is deter-mining what is, and is not, feng shui. The burgeoning of all kinds of feng shui schools has led to some confusion over this but, as with all good things, situations eventually crystallize into a harmonious balance. When you find the real feng shui, it will amaze you with stunning results.

The celestial creatures

"Where there is found the azure dragon, there too shall be the white tiger, coiled in tight embrace. The earth's forces indicate harmony when all things else appear in balance. Behold the dragon's cosmic breath; in such a place, build your home."

The green dragon is the most powerful celestial creature in Chinese feng shui. The other three powerful animals are the white tiger, the red phoenix, and the black tortoise. These celestial creatures are regarded as auspicious symbols in and of themselves, with each creature symbolizing something beneficial to mankind's luck.

The green dragon, which is the celestial creature of the East, is the most powerful embodiment of beneficial energy, and its cosmic breath, or chi, is the all-pervasive force that brings good fortune.

This chi swirls benevolently around the environment and, wherever it exists in large quantities, it is said to be the resting place of the dragon. Such places are usually areas that appear undulating rather than flat, with graduated contours rather than a series of sharp peaks. Land that is completely flat does not have dragons and is said to be inauspicious. Land that undulates, where dragons reside is said to be auspicious.

The Chinese believe that natural environments, which signify the presence of the true dragon, also have a white tiger close by. When these two celestial creatures are locked in copulation, an abundance of celestial dragon's cosmic breath gets released. Such auspicious places are said to be where the dragon dwells in blissful contentment.

To identify such places successfully requires experience in assessing the natural forms and topography of the land. Only certain types of contours can represent the green dragon and white tiger formations.

Experienced masters add two other creatures to make identification easier – the black tortoise behind and the red phoenix in front.

The tortoise is represented by a hill that resembles its back – round, like a hump. A tortoise hill provides shelter for the dragon and tiger and gives support behind you. There are many old-time feng shui masters who stubbornly maintain that having a tortoise hill behind

The celestial animals of the green dragon, the white tiger, the black tortoise, and the red phoenix relate to environmental feng shui. The tortoise is a hump-backed hill, the dragon higher mountains than the tiger, and the phoenix elevated ground.

Directions of the Celestial Creatures

your house is even more important than having the dragon-tiger formation!

In addition, they point to the presence of the crimson bird, or red phoenix, which brings opportunities to all those who live in correct orientation to it. This celestial creature usually takes the shape and form of a small hillock or elevated ground in front of the tortoise hill.

LANDSCAPE FENG SHUI

These four celestial creatures collectively embody the essence of landscape, or environmental, feng shui. This is the older school of feng shui, which analyzes the shape of mountains and the flow of rivers. In addition to hills and mountains taking on the symbolism of the four celestial creatures, they also have yin and yang aspects and exhibit element characteristics. Thus, dragon and tiger mountains may have portions of their terrain that resemble any one of the five elemental shapes. So fire-dragon mountains tend to have sharper peaks and more jagged edges, while water-dragon mountains tend to be made up of a series of hills that resemble waves. Square plateau-type elevations signify earth-dragon mountains, round hills indicate metal-dragon mountains, and steep elevations indicate wood-dragon mountains.

These sub-categories of mountain shapes offer a fine tuning of landscape features, which experienced masters use to predict the

In relation to the compass, the tortoise is in the north, the dragon in the east, the tiger in the west, and phoenix in the south, but, in practice, you can regard the higher land on the left side of the home as the dragon side, and the right side as the tiger side.

fortunes of families. Much of their analysis combines knowledge of compass-formula readings as well, which often give accurate feng shui analysis of what will happen to a family's fortunes, as well as the destiny of each of its children. The presence of mountain peaks and hill ranges in the vicinity of homes can hold different meanings, depending on the orientations of these natural features.

THE BEST ORIENTATION FOR THE HOME

To get the best out of the four celestial creatures, the general rules concerning orientation are to make sure that tortoise hills are always behind your home, since these provide much-needed support. The land behind any home should, therefore, be higher ground. A hump-backed hill immediately behind a house is considered to be an auspicious feature of support. When a hill or mountain lies directly before your front door, the general consensus is that your luck is permanently blocked. It is like confronting a mountain – a situation that signifies danger. If the hill in front of your home is further away from the main door and is not overly big, then it does not represent harm, but is, in fact, quite auspicious, since this signifies the phoenix.

Meanwhile, the land on your left-hand side (when standing at the front door and looking out) is said to represent the green dragon. The dragon side should always be higher than the tiger on the right-hand side. This ensures that the green dragon is more important than the white tiger.

In recent times, feng shui masters have used the symbolism of the four celestial creatures to suggest ways to create their essence in the home. This is especially applicable for those who live in high-rise apartments. Therefore, it is a good idea to place a dragon image on the east side of your living room; a red bird in the south; and a tortoise in the north. This is believed to bring the chi of these celestial creatures into the home. The tiger has been left out because not everyone is able to sustain the aggressive chi of this animal. While tiger images are appropriate – and even auspicious – in homes where the patriarch was born in either a dragon or tiger year, anyone born in a small-animal year could well succumb to the ferocity of the tiger.

"A hump-backed hill immediately behind the house is considered to be an auspicious feature of support."

Chi: the dragon's cosmic breath

As we have seen, the dragon's cosmic breath is the beneficial energy that swirls around the environment – this is the magical life force that pervades every place in the universe. Almost all Chinese physical skills that deal with the environment, human endurance, and creativity describe the importance of this life force.

"I am strength and courage, the bearer of good fortune.
I am power and determination, the source of good energy.
I am the messenger of good tidings.
When dark clouds disappear, I bring growth in abundance.
I am the mighty dragon's cosmic breath."

In feng shui, natural environments that have an abundance of this chi are highly prized, but experience is required to identify them. To start with, it is essential to understand that beneficial chi moves slowly; it never moves too fast. Beneficial chi meanders; it never moves in a straight line. In places where there is a good balance of yin and yang energy, it tends to settle and accumulate. Chi also requires the air to be fresh and clean. When the atmosphere gets too damp, too wet, too dry, or too hot, chi becomes stale; when a place gets dirty, chi turns insipid.

Beneficial chi brings strength, vigor, and good fortune. It is vibrant and full of energy. It is different from the wind, yet it travels with the wind. It exists in the air, under the ground, in water, and within the human body itself.

Mankind chi is life energy that gives focused strength to martial arts' exponents and imparts special skills to artists. And Chinese healing methods are based on diagnosing for blockages in the flow of chi within the human body.

In feng shui, when three doors are in a straight line in the home, they are thought to represent bad luck, as the chi energy flows too swiftly through them.

FENG SHUI TABOOS

In feng shui, the chi that flows around a home should never be blocked. When plumbing does not work, it should be fixed immediately. When drains get blocked, the luck of the family will deteriorate. The design of doors and windows, which lead the flow of chi from room to room within a home, should always cause the flow to meander. Chi should never be allowed to flow in a straight line.

When chi gathers speed, it turns malicious. For this reason, a major taboo in feng shui is the configuration of two or three doors in a straight line. Three doors especially, with one opening onto another, represents bad luck — especially when one of the doors is the main front door and the other is the back door.

A variation of this is a mirror that directly reflects the main door, which causes chi to enter the home but fly straight out again. So, while mirrors are a panacea for many feng shui ills, they must be installed carefully. Mirrors must never reflect the main door.

Chi is said to stop and settle when it encounters water. For this reason, water features are said to be auspicious. In feng shui, water also represents money, and the presence of water in the vicinity of a home tends to bring good luck through the front door. But water must be oriented correctly in order to tap its benefits.

Physical features of the environment affect the intrinsic nature of chi. Whether it is auspicious or not depends on how encircling hills and mountains are oriented. When these structures encourage chi to settle, the effect is good; when they encourage it to dissipate, the effect is bad. Man-made structures also affect the flow of chi. When buildings, roads, and highways blend harmoniously with natural surroundings, the flow of chi is enhanced and its beneficial qualities are magnified. When it encounters sharp or angular structures, chi takes on hostile stamina and transforms itself into harmful energy. Beneficial chi is termed sheng chi; harmful chi is termed shar chi.

"Beneficial chi is termed sheng chi, while harmful chi is termed shar chi."

THE EFFECT OF ROADS

From a feng shui perspective, it is a good idea to avoid living at the end of a road, where chi is said to stagnate. If your luck changes for the worse, this kind of configuration magnifies your bad-luck situation, as it symbolizes no way out of your problems. Usually when you are going through a good period, living in a dead end will not create any problems, but when you are going through a tough time, it compounds bad luck. It is also not beneficial to live in a one-level house that is sandwiched between two multi-level, imposing homes. The houses next to you will block the flow of benevolent chi towards your house, adversely affecting your well-being and your luck.

Living in a one-storey house that is situated between two larger properties is not ideal, as the flow of good chi is blocked.

The same rule applies to commercial buildings in the city. To correct this, you should place a bright light shining upwards.

Another sound suggestion is to avoid living in a building that directly faces an oncoming straight road. This forms the classical T-junction, regarded as so harmful that the bad chi that enters your home is said to be a killer – its effect is lethal. An excellent example of this configuration is London's Buckingham Palace, which directly faces the long avenue known as the Mall. Here the straight road sends horrible shar chi towards the palace, adversely affecting the happiness of the residents within. Thankfully, there is a huge round-about just in front of the palace gates, which successfully deflects some of the deadly, killing energy.

You can deal with T-junctions by planting some trees or building a wall to block off the road, or by changing your main door, so that the road hits a wall rather than your entrance. However, T-junctions and straight roads do not harm you when the house sits on elevated land. The deadly chi cannot harm homes that are located higher than the road. On the other hand, when the house sits on land that is lower than the road, it becomes necessary to raise the chi of the home symbolically with strategically placed lights. Better still, build another level to the house, so that the roof level is higher than the road. Or do both!

Chi that stays below road level is never auspicious. For this reason, overseas Chinese who emigrate to Western countries usually avoid basement flats, unless there is a level garden to compensate for the below-road-level flat. Even then, sleeping below road level can cause residents to suffer from bad-fortune chi.

Understanding the way that chi moves offers clues to the way in which roads can affect the feng shui of a home. Generally it is not a good idea to live excessively close to roads and highways with fast-moving traffic. Like the traffic, chi will also move too fast, bringing misfortune. However, it is considered good luck to be located near busy roads with slow-moving traffic, as long as there are no traffic jams. Those living in residential areas usually benefit from being away from fast-moving traffic, unless there is a flyover nearby. Elevated roadways can cause horrible feng shui, so if you live too close by, my suggestion is to plant tall trees between your house and the highway.

Top: It is best to avoid living in a house that is opposite a T-junction, as shar chi directly affects it. If you have no choice, plant some trees to filter the bad energy.
Above: If a house is positioned on a bend, it will fare better if it is inside the curve, as the road will embrace it.

When there is a curve in the road in front of the house, it is better to be on the inside of the curve than on the outside. When the house is located outside the curve, the road becomes a knife that symbolically cuts into the house. The chi at this side of the road is malevolent, while the chi on the other side is usually benevolent. The road should embrace the house.

The lo shu square on the
back of a turtle

Many thousands of eons ago, a turtle is said to have emerged from the River Lo in China carrying on his back a pattern of dots, which eventually became the magical Lo Shu square that unlocked the secrets of the Pa Kua. When you understand the significance of this, it is not surprising that so many of feng shui's most potent formulas depend on the correct application of this square.

"It was the turtle that brought the Lo Shu square on its back — a square that has since provided the key to decoding the eight-sided Pa Kua."

*I*n 1989, shortly after my retirement from the corporate world, I went to Pangkor island with my family and came across a turtle shell 50cm/18in in length. It was very beautiful and at a subconscious level something registered, but it was only last year, while going through some family holiday pictures, that I recalled the discovery. Since then, of course, I have become the world's best-selling writer on feng shui. Surely discovering that turtle shell all those years ago was more a sign of things to come than a coincidence?

The turtle, or tortoise, is an important creature in feng shui. It is the only one of the four "celestial creatures" that exists, for the other three – the dragon, the phoenix, and the unicorn (white tiger) – are legendary rather than real (see p. 100). The turtle is also a much-revered auspicious symbol of support. Most importantly, it was the turtle that brought the Lo Shu square on its back thousands of years ago – a square that has since provided the key to decoding the eight-sided Pa Kua.

The legend explains that nine numbers, in the form of dots, had been arranged on the back of the turtle into a three-by-three grid pattern. The numbers were placed in such a way that adding them up in any direction – lengthwise, sideways, or diagonally – always gave the same number: fifteen. The significance of the number fifteen is that this is the number of days it takes for the moon to complete one waxing or waning cycle, suggesting that there might be a time correlation between the pattern of numbers and the Pa Kua, as well as a correlation with the Chinese calendar. This grid eventually became the Lo Shu square.

The arrangement of the numbers into a nine-chamber grid in three lines came to exert a powerful and mythical influence on Chinese cultural symbolism. Eventually the pattern of numbers came to be irretrievably associated with the trigrams of the Later Heaven Pa Kua. More importantly, the Lo Shu square became the basis of much of Taoism's magical practices. Thus, many Taoist rituals today still continue to be synchronized in accordance with the way the Lo Shu numbers interacted with the Hsia calendar.

The two powerful feng shui formulas in use today are based on the Lo Shu square. Flying Star and Eight Mansions feng shui both require a thorough understanding of the way the numbers "move" around the Lo Shu grid, and of the different ways in which the Lo Shu interacts with the eight trigrams, the elements, and the directions of the compass.

THE LO SHU SYMBOL
Academic study of the pattern of numbers on the Lo Shu square concentrates on the striking similarities between the way that the grid's numbers move and the symbol that is created. For instance, the sign that is formed strongly resembles the ancient Hebrews' reputedly powerful Sigil of Saturn sign. Any connection with this is, of course, speculative, but the fact remains that the sign created by the movement of the numbers does resemble the sigil.

The movement and the sign, illustrated here, hold the key to unlocking many of the secrets of Flying Star feng shui, which reveals the auspicious and inauspicious corners of any residence or building. It also identifies the flight of good and bad stars each year.

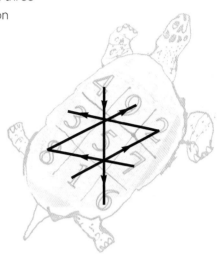

Above: The way the numbers move creates a symbol that is used in Flying Star feng shui.
Below: The turtle is a revered animal in feng shui. This is because, according to legend, a turtle came out of the River Lo in China with a pattern of dots of its back which became the numbers of the magical Lo Shu square.

The eight mansions
kua formula

Feng shui is earth luck at its most effecive, and Eight Mansions feng shui is one of the most potent techniques in use today. The Eight Mansions formula highlights east- and west-house theories of feng shui. This compass method is easy to learn and apply, and it can be very powerfully potent to those who use it correctly and diligently.

*T*his powerful compass-school formula taken from the classical texts offers a personalized method for determining the most auspicious directions and locations (as well as the inauspicious ones) according to birth dates and gender. Its great value lies in its tremendous potency, the speed with which it works, and its incredible ease of use. The formula is simple to apply, but there are different ways of using it. Indeed, I have written an entire book on this formula alone, because there are so many permutations and it has so much feng shui relevance.

In this book, all that I can do is teach you how to determine your personal good-fortune directions and warn you against inauspicious directions. To get the most out of the Eight Mansions formula, you should really go much deeper into its study.

To determine your personal auspicious and inauspicious directions, you need first to work out your personal KUA number. The calculation of this requires your year of birth and your gender. Your year of birth must be adjusted to fit the Chinese calendar. In order to be exact, one should take note of the start of the lunar year each year to make this adjust-

THE FORMULA FOR MEN

Take your year of birth; add the last two digits together and keep adding them until you get a single digit. Then deduct the result from 10. For those born in the year 2000 and beyond, deduct the result from 9 instead of 10.

Example: year of birth 1936, so 3 + 6 = 9, and 10 - 9 = 1, so your KUA number is 1.

Example: year of birth 2000, so 0 + 0 = 0, and 9 - 0 = 9, so your KUA number is 9.

THE FORMULA FOR WOMEN

Take your year of birth; add the last two digits together, and keep adding them until you get a single digit. Then add 5; if you get two digits, then add them together to get a single digit. For those born in the year 2000 and beyond, add 6 instead of 5.

Example: year of birth 1945, so 4 + 5 = 9, and 9 + 5 = 14; 1 + 4 = 5, so your KUA number is 5.

Example: year of birth 2000, so 0 + 0 = 0, and 0 + 6 = 6, so your KUA number is 6.

ment, but many masters also use the Hsia calendar, which uses February 4 as the start date for the Chinese New Year. For instance, if you were born on February 3, 1973, you should use 1972 as your year of birth; if you were born on February 4, you should use 1973.

Once you have discovered your KUA number from the formula above, you will be able to discover whether you are an east-group person or a west-group person. According to this method of feng shui, everyone belongs to one of these groupings. Generally east-group people are extremely compatible with other east-group people and extremely incompatible with west-group people; and likewise for west-group people. To find out whether you are an east- or west-group person, all you have to do is match your KUA number to the groups given below:

● East-group people have KUA numbers 1, 3, 4, and 9 and their auspicious directions are east, south-east, north, and south.
● West-group people have KUA numbers 2, 5, 6, 7, and 8 and their auspicious directions are the west, the south-west, the north-west and, the north-east.

According to this formula, there are four lucky and four unlucky directions for each person. As a general aid to daily living, you should remember that, if you are an east-group person, your lucky directions are the east-group ones and your unlucky directions are the west-group ones. On the other hand, if you are a west-group person, your lucky directions are the west-group ones and your unlucky directions are the east-group ones.

Luck from the
ten directions

"So what are the ten directions?" a student asked me. "I see only eight directions." Of course he was forgetting that, in addition to the compass points, there is also the luck from above and the luck from below.

$\mathcal{E}$arth luck comes from all directions – as much from the four cardinal and secondary directions as from above and below. In truth, you determine the quality of your heaven luck and earth luck. Heaven luck is karma, determined by actions in previous lives; mankind luck is determined by your actions in this life. Luck from above and below can negate the good luck you have created from the eight directions, or it can enhance it. We are in command of our earth and mankind luck, and together we can arrange our living space, create a mental attitude, and adopt a way of living that can enhance whatever good heaven luck we have brought into this lifetime.

Feng shui cannot completely wipe out karmic forces, but, with a good heart and right motivations, we can transform an ordinary life into an exemplary, even stunning one.

EAST-GROUP PEOPLE

KUA numbers	1	3	4	9
Best success direction	south-east	south	north	east
Best health direction	east	north	south	south-east
Best romance direction	south	south-east	east	north
Personal growth direction	north	east	south-east	south
Unlucky direction	west	south-west	north-west	north-east
Five Ghosts direction	north-east	north-west	south-west	west
Six Killings direction	north-west	north-east	west	south-west
Total loss direction	south-west	west	north-east	north-west

Based on the Eight Mansions formula, each direction brings different types of luck, and represents a specific type of good or bad luck. Each of the KUA numbers allows this to be spelled out. In revealing the intensity of good or bad luck for each direction, this compass formula can help you fine-tune your feng shui. The directions have many applications, the most obvious being the orientation of the main and secondary doors, the sleeping direction and location, the eating direction, the working direction and location, and the travel direction.

You can, therefore, use the Eight Mansions formula to activate particular aspirations. It does not matter if you are a west- or east-group person. The way to activate a direction is to make sure that you are using the direction that is suited to the kind of luck you want, based on your date of birth and your KUA number. So, for success at work, sit at your desk directly facing your best direction. For health problems, sleep with your head pointing in your health direction, and eat facing your health direction. If you wish to study better and improve your exam grades, position your desk facing your personal growth direction and try to take your exams facing in that direction.

BEST DIRECTIONS

● If for some reason you are unable to sleep, sit, or work facing the direction you want to (and this is quite likely), then try to tap into at least one of your four auspicious directions. This is to ensure that you do not sit or sleep, work or study, facing any of your inauspicious directions – two of which can be deadly indeed. The Six Killings and the Total Loss direction are to be feared, since they are considered malevolent.

WEST-GROUP PEOPLE

KUA numbers	5	5	2	6	7	8
	male	female	all	all	all	all
Best success direction	north-east	south-west	north-east	west	north-west	south-west
Best health direction	west	north-west	west	north-east	south-west	north-west
Best romance direction	north-west	west	north-west	south-west	north-east	west
Personal growth direction	south-west	north-west	south-west	north-west	west	north-east
Unlucky direction	east	south	east	south-east	north	south
Five Ghosts direction	south-east	north	south-east	east	south	north
Six Killings direction	south	east	south	north	south-east	east
Total Loss direction	north	south-east	north	south	east	south-east

Productive & destructive cycles of the five elements

By taking an object and recognizing its intrinsic qualitative attributes, we can categorize it as belonging to the fire, water, earth, wood, or metal element, since everything in the universe belongs to one of these elemental energy manifestations.

*T*he theory of the Five Elements is intrinsic to all branches of Chinese divination. From astrological fortune-telling to oracle forecasting, through the *I Ching*, understanding the productive and destructive cycles of the Five Elements – how they interact with each other to create positive, auspicious energy or negative, inauspicious energy – is what offers potency to the practice.

In feng shui, the attributes of the elements influence each of the eight sectors of the compass. The four cardinal and four secondary directions each have a corresponding element. Therefore, the easy way to create positive feng shui is simply to energize the element of each compass sector. So understanding element attributes is essential.

Feng shui contends that everything in the universe possesses intangible energies that have elemental connotations. Thus, seasons, colors, shapes, directions of energy flows, and even numbers have element equivalents. Studying element symbolism is, hence, an essential component of feng shui practice. Feng shui masters commit the elemental attributes and associations to memory, because applications of element theory lie behind many of the diagnoses offered and cures suggested. A great many of the feng shui enhancing techniques also have their roots in the Five Elements (in Chinese termed *wu xing*) of fire, wood, water, metal, and earth.

1 *Fire*
The Ultimate Yang Element

Fire is an extremely powerful element, but it does not exist of itself – it has to be created. Unlike the other elements, fire cannot be stored. Fire energy offers success in public life and brings fame, recognition, and shining achievement to those who successfully activate its energies. But fire must be kept under control at all times, for an excess of fire energy may be fatal. Fire is associated with the south.

2 *Water*
The Wealth Energy

Like fire, water is an extremely powerful element, which can get out of control. Water energy moves downwards, so, when it overflows, it creates destruction and loss. It also brings prosperity, and if you energize it correctly and in proper alignment with the other energies, so that there is an auspicious balance, water energy will make you rich beyond your expectations. Water is identified with the north.

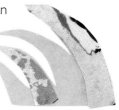

3 *Earth*
The Grounding Energy

Earth epitomizes the core of feng shui. Tapping earth luck brings harmony and great family happiness, usually associated with the efforts of the matriarch. Earth is the element that dominates the south-west, the north-east, and the central grid of a home.

4 *Wood*
The Growth Energy

Wood brings expansion and advancement, and its energies bring material success. Like the branches of a tree, good luck grows ever outward – wood being the only element that has life. Wood energy also confers excellent descendants luck on families, and is especially beneficial to the sons of the family. Wood is the direction of the east and the south-east.

5 *Metal*
The Energy of Power

Metal brings the luck of powerful and helpful people: what the Chinese term "heaven men." It symbolizes the strength of heaven and the power of the patriarch. Metal is always associated with gold and silver, and its energy is dense and inward-flowing. Metal energies are unbending and resolute, but if you successfully tap into the auspicious metal energy, your life will be one of great influence. One of the least-known, yet most potent, methods of attracting this energy is to hang a tiny golden bell in the north-west corner of your home to activate

THE ELEMENTS AND THEIR ASSOCIATIONS

Element	wood	water	fire	metal	earth
Season	spring	winter	summer	fall	between
Direction	east/south-east	north	south	west/north-west	south-west/north-east
Color	green	blue/black	red	white	ocher
Shape	rectangle	wavy	triangular	round	square
Energy	upward	descending	outward	inward	sideways
Numbers	3, 4	1	9	6, 7	2, 5, 8

the luck of having many helpful people in your life. Metal is the element of the west and the north-west.

Other attributes of the Five Elements that are useful to remember, and which are often incorporated into fortune-telling and feng shui analysis, are summarized in the table above. Use these additional attributes for further analysis and creativity in practice.

The concept of *wu xing*, or the Five Elements, can also mean five types of activity, for the word *wu* means "five," while *xing* is the expression of chi dominating at different times.

Water dominates in winter, wood in spring, fire in summer, and metal in autumn. At the intersection between two seasons, the transitional period is dominated by earth. The terms "water," "wood," "fire," "metal," and "earth" refer to substances whose properties resemble the respective chi and help us understand the different properties of the five types of chi.

The properties of these five types of chi are summarized as follows:
● Water: runs downward, so there is always danger of an overflow
● Wood: grows upward, and is an excellent representation of life and growth
● Fire: spreads in all directions – radiant, hot, and has a tendency to get out of control
● Metal: piercing inwards – sharp, pointing, and can be deadly powerful
● Earth: attracts and nourishes – stable, caring, and protective.

In addition, it is useful to know that the element metal encompasses minerals, hydrogen and other elements. Wood encompasses all plant life. Plant life is rooted to the earth, grows from the earth, and is constantly alive in one form or another in the earth. Wood, therefore, becomes the symbol of life. The fire element encompasses heat – light, the digestive process, anger, and so on. Water encompasses all liquid manifestations of energy, and it suggests the quality of yielding to force. At the center is Earth, which is then seen as the great equalizer, the balancer of all forces, the sustainer of life.

Element analysis uncovers multiple layers of meaning. It features strongly in the analysis of individuals' Four Pillars charts and in the feng shui natal chart of any abode. For anyone to become a master in either of these esoteric practices, a deep understanding of the interacting energies of the Five Elements is vital.

When feng shui consultants work with the Five Elements, they need to know the Productive and Destructive Element cycle well. For example, in the Productive Cycle, fire feeds earth, so lights or red accessories in the south of a room will draw fame or personal success into your life.

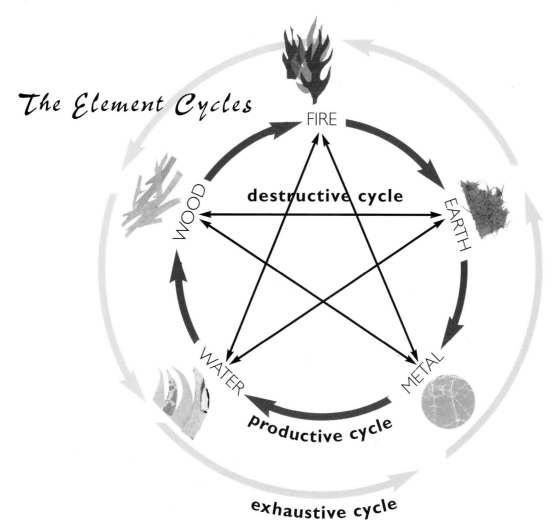

The Element Cycles

FIRE

WOOD

destructive cycle

EARTH

WATER

METAL

productive cycle

exhaustive cycle

Harnessing the power of
wind and water

"Water flows gently, yet over time it has the power to conquer the highest mountain. And water at its zenith quickly changes from benevolence into an element of danger."

The Chinese have a healthy respect for the good and bad qualities of water. As one of the Five Elements, it is recognized as having the potential to bring immense good fortune but also extreme misfortune. Water flows in rivers and seas, and seeps relentlessly into the earth, quietly eroding away, infiltrating and restructuring things that stand in its path.

Water can also roar like a deluge, putting out fires and flooding the land, destroying everything in its path. Thus the element of water can suggest subtle and gentle persistence, like the brook successfully wearing away the hardest rocks, or it can be like rust destroying steel bars over time. Water is fluid and flexible, seeping through the tiniest pores and covering the largest of surface areas. Water may be a rivulet or it may be the great ocean.

In feng shui, water represents both great danger and enormous wealth. As an element, it can be said to be most extreme and, because of this, is always given extra care, particularly as it pertains to the direction of earth luck. Orientations of homes that are built near large bodies of water or of major water courses are always carefully worked out so that the very best of this element is tapped. Water inside the home is also carefully placed to make the best of the space's chi.

It is said that the sheng chi that brings good fortune stops when it is confronted with water, and water above a mountain or in high places is one of the four danger signs of the I Ching. And yet, water almost always offers potential for good fortune.

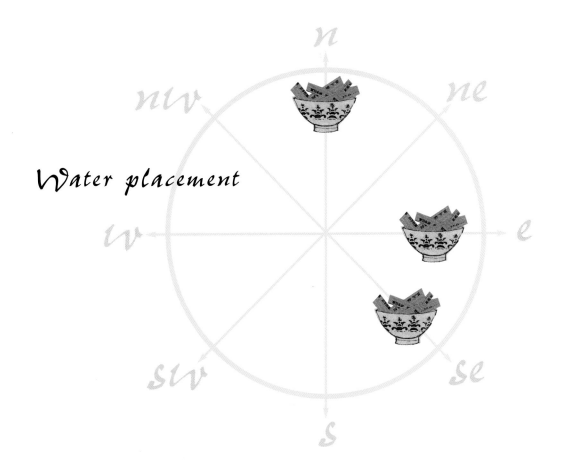

Water placement

WATER PEOPLE

People born of the water element (those whose birth charts contain a dominance of water) are usually excellent communicators. They are charming, likeable, and often extremely persuasive, relentlessly wearing down the most obstinate resistance. They are tenacious, but they can also compromise to an extent that suggests weakness. Their attitude to life is flexible and they prefer the soft approach.

The water element always adds a calming influence, so that aggressive and hostile behavior often becomes modified under the influence of water, just as passionate and emotional natures are cooled by the water symbol.

The way of the water element is to infiltrate rather than dominate. Water people are also effective catalysts and have a knack for knowing the best people to approach to solve any given problem, the best time to start any project, and the most effective indirect way of getting things done. They are usually passive and conciliatory, and often adopt the simplest course of action.

The water element has the potential to bring good fortune, but must be used carefully. Water relates to the north so can be placed in that part of the home, it can also be set in the east (wood) and south-east (wood), as water feeds wood in the Productive Cycle.

Water is usually an excellent additional element for those born under the influence of wood, since water enables plants to grow and flourish. But too much water can cause the roots to rot and plants to die. Balance is important. Water is usually not good for those born under the influence of the fire element, but when there is too much fire in the birth chart, water becomes an effective balancing agent. For those born with a preponderance of water in their birth chart, metal is good, and metal-dominated people will suit them. Wearing gold accessories and carrying lots of coins is therefore, beneficial for them. But earth people will take advantage of their good nature.

If you need to enhance your fortunes or your relationships with water, wear the colors blue or black; drink plenty of water daily; and try to live near a river or a lake. But don't overdo it by having too much water! And if you want to use water to enhance the feng shui of your home, always place water in the north, east, or south-east — never in the south, west, or north-west.

One of the most popular symbols of business success leading to the accumulation of wealth, which was favored by Chinese merchant traders in South-East Asia at the start of the nineteenth century, was the merchant ship. Many used a junk or a sailing ship laden with cargo as their business logo, and with great success. The sailing ship signifies a bountiful cargo brought to you by the waters and fuelled by the wind — wind and water being the two auspicious forces that propel feng shui.

The sailing ship is, thus symbolically, a most auspicious object, but, to be truly lucky, the wealth ship should be piled high with gold ingots, in order to bring greater income and success to your business. The gold ingots need not be real gold, although naturally there is nothing like the real thing!

My advice has always been to have a dozen imitation gold ingots on standby at home. These may be used in dozens of ways to create auspicious earth luck, but one way is to place them inside model sailing ships: look for a ship that is well made, from hardwood, and with full sails in place (the sails capture the wind). A ship about 30cm/12in long would be an ideal wealth object.

Place the model ship in your office, preferably in the foyer area of the building. Position it correctly, since it must look as if it is sailing into the office and not sailing out (if the ship is sailing out, you will lose

"One of the most popular symbols of business success leading to the accumulation of wealth, which was favored by Chinese merchant traders in South-East Asia at the start of the nineteenth century, was the merchant ship loaded with gold."

money). Check that this is so by looking at the sails. Let it seem as if the wind is blowing the ship forcefully into harbor – in whichever room the ship is placed, that will be the harbor. For it to have a really positive meaning, the ship should be laden with gold.

Alternatively, you can choose to place the ship within your house, preferably set on a low table. If you are greedy for more wealth, of course you can have more than one ship, therefore making your house into a real "harbor," with each ship representing a different source of income! Many ships will, therefore, mean that you have numerous sources of income.

A sailing ship is considered an auspicious object, as it signifies a bountiful cargo being brought to you. If you use one in your home or office, make sure it is a good hardwood design, fill it with artificial gold ingots, and place it on a small table or in your foyer, making sure that the sails are the right way round for sailing in.

Three friends in winter: how to be a brilliant survivor

The wise man (or woman) who is able to overcome all obstacles and make a success of living is one whose spontaneous attitude resembles the qualities of the pine tree, the plum blossom, and the bamboo. These are the three "friends" in winter – the attitudes that we need to survive with dignity.

In Taoist wisdom, there are thought to be three "friends" in winter – that is attitudes we need to be successful. The first is the dignity of the pine tree, the second is the wisdom of the plum blossom, and the third is the endurance of the bamboo.

Success comes from the matchless wisdom of cultivating a proper attitude toward others in your daily affairs and toward the whole circumstance of your life. The wise man (or woman) who is able to overcome all obstacles and make a success of living is one whose spontaneous attitude "resembles the three friends in winter" – these are the pine tree, the plum blossom, and the bamboo.

1 *The dignity of the pine tree*
Fairness Brings Good Fortune

The wise person stays calm, relaxed, and unruffled by circumstance, and works at being pleasantly accommodating, irrespective of the weather or the nature of the situation. He or she strives never to take offense, but instead cultivates good humor and is rarely, if ever, overwhelmed either by small hiccups in life or by major adversity. According to Taoist precepts, this attitude is what attracts the matchless blessing of good health and long life. Such an approach resembles the upright pine tree, which stands erect and tall, regardless of the time of year. Pine trees are perceived as being equally happy and amazingly evergreen throughout the year. In the sunshine of summer or the intense cold of winter, the pine stands unperturbed. It is regarded as the first friend of winter.

2 *The wisdom of the plum blossom*
Tranquillity Leads To Determination

The wise person also cultivates the ability to bloom in the midst of misfortune, resembling the plum blossom, whose crimson petals gleam brilliantly against the white snows of winter. The plum blossom demonstrates beauty and serenity and is supremely unaffected by the chill of cold and dreary weather. This suggests a tranquillity of mind that is said to lead to an attitude of forbearance, so that, even in difficult times and circumstances, the ability to survive, to perform, and even to shine stays intact. The plum blossom is the second friend in winter.

3 *The endurance of the bamboo*
Flexibility Means No Hostility

According to Taoist adepts, however, the most important attitude for success is one characterized by the third friend in winter – the bamboo, which is soft and supple, yet at the same time strong and hardy. The bamboo is a friend because it is flexible, able to bend according to the prevailing winds, capable of adapting to circumstances, and never hurt by adverse conditions. Far from being broken, the bamboo has the resilience to bounce back from bad times. This attitude leads to a flexible disposition, which introduces goodwill into every potential situation of conflict or hostility.

"Like the pine tree, the sage hopes to achieve longevity. Like the plum blossom, he flowers in adversity. And like the bamboo, he bends to accommodate the prevailing winds of circumstance before springing back with effortless resilience. These are the three friends of winter."

The highest technique of survival strategy is always to win without fighting; this is because in every confrontation situation all sides stand to lose something. There can be little peace of mind or good health when your attitude is aggressive. Far better to be like the bamboo and adjust naturally to the winds of the moment, conserving your energy and waiting for a less hostile situation, before springing back from a position of strength.

Implied in this morsel of Taoist wisdom is that it is better to ride with the flow and swim with the current than move against them. Energy is conserved when you do not battle against the tide. It is easier to go, round a stone than bash your head against it; wiser to circumvent something than press on against insurmountable odds. The true hero is the one who looks for the line of least resistance. This does not imply a surrender of your objectives, or abandonment of your goals or principles – it is just that it is far wiser to preserve your energy and resources than try to fight an impossible war or adversary.

SYMBOL OF LONGEVITY

The bamboo is a legendary symbol of longevity: it survives and grows stronger with each passing season. When conditions are fertile, it thrives, enjoying the good times with no clinging attachment. When the soil turns arid and the weather becomes unfriendly, it conserves its strength, accepting the harsher conditions with equanimity and therefore surviving. In the same way, the wise person understands that there can be no summer without winter, no ups without downs, no growth without decay. How resilient you are depends in the end on your perceptions and your attitude to circumstances. When you are like the three friends in winter, you take everything in your stride, in tranquillity, putting forth energy when needed, yet always staying inwardly relaxed. This is the secret of living to a ripe old age.

The bamboo is one of the most celebrated plants in Chinese art and culture, and is said to be able to live more than a thousand years. It is celebrated for its color, the slenderness of its appearance and, most of all, for its ability to bend without breaking – the very qualities of a Taoist or Confucian scholar. The young bamboo shoot is a popular food at Chinese dining tables, while its pith is a much sought-after and an expensive delicacy. It is delicious in taste and texture and is said to possess medicinal qualities, as it is cooling to the body system. The bamboo is also a popular subject of artists and artisans; scholars are regarded as accomplished only when they are able either to paint or compose a couplet on the merits of the bamboo.

The bamboo is the third "friend" in winter and is also the symbol of longevity, as it grows stronger each season. To resemble the bamboo and live to an old age, you need to be flexible and relaxed, exerting energy only when needed.

Ancient scholars wrote their memoirs and thoughts on strips of bamboo, which were then bundled together, tied with red cloth, and carefully locked away:

> *"Every little word*
> *on every little strip of bamboo*
> *echoes deeply inside me*
> *reflects my mind*
> *at each moment of time.*
> *Reflections of Sun Tzu"*

In feng shui, bamboo is highly prized as a symbol of good health and longevity. Growing a small clump in the front garden or hanging a painting of bamboo in the living room is said to be most auspicious. But bamboo paintings should always demonstrate the strength of the brushstrokes. It is believed that only a highly accomplished artist or calligrapher can execute a painting of bamboo that has true auspicious value, and only then will the brushstrokes contain the highly prized chi, or cosmic breath, that brings good health and fortune.

Taoist meditative techniques

"True wisdom arises from wordless teaching. Learning from books can sometimes be an impediment to progress, yet books are often invaluable in showing the mind where to start and where to turn."

"My lama said to me once, 'Lillian, meditation is such a wonderful practice, there surely must be a higher purpose to meditation than merely to attain relaxation'."

There are two types of meditation: formal and casual. In formal meditation, the motivation is always made clear, so that the mind is able to focus single-mindedly on the object (and subject) of contemplation. Sitting, breathing deeply, and cultivating stillness of mind are the three prerequisites for this kind of meditative exercise.

Casual meditation is considered equally beneficial and may be done while taking a stroll, waiting in line, sitting quietly, or lying down prior to falling asleep. Anyone can practise this sort of contemplation, and yogic benefits will definitely accrue. I want to advise readers that conversations I have had with advanced Taoist masters have reassured me that, while it is wonderful to be able to sit cross-legged with the soles of the feet facing upwards, like the Buddha, this is not a prerequisite for progress.

The lotus posture is an effective aid to attaining proper breathing, which promotes the circulation of chi within the body. Raising the chi is what enables the mind to relax and transcend into altered states of consciousness. It is important to cultivate both proper sitting positions and the correct posture.

However, when you are a beginner and doing meditative yoga for the first time, and you are unable to retain the lotus posture due to aches arising from being in the posture for too long, then it is far better to practise contemplative yoga casually – you can do this while sitting down or while you are out strolling. Becoming relaxed is far more important in the early stages than controlling the breathing and the movement of chi inside the body.

THE LOTUS POSTURE

While meditation masters will insist that you should sit in a pre-scribed manner to make progress, the lotus position is really only ideal for serious meditation if you can maintain it without discomfort.

1 *Body position*
Moving into the Lotus

If you cannot sit like a Buddha (cross-legged on the ground, with the soles of both feet facing upwards), start by just crossing your legs; then move to the half-lotus (in which the sole of one foot faces upwards) before eventually trying the full lotus. You will find that it is a lot easier when you place a small, round cushion underneath you to raise your buttocks, since this reduces the pressure on your legs. The taller or bigger you are, the higher this cushion should be. If you want something harder, you might like to use a small wooden stool instead. The main thing is to feel comfortable so that you can relax.

2 *Hand positions*
Making a Mudra

Different Buddhist masters use different hand positions or "mudras," but you might wish to try resting your hands lightly on your lap and in some form of contact with each other. Try cupping your right hand in the palm of your left hand. Let the right thumb face upwards and the knuckles rest lightly on the palm of the left hand. Hold your body straight, but stay relaxed at all times – try not to go rigid. Incline your head very slightly forwards and keep your eyes slightly open.

3 *Mouth position*
Teeth and Tongue

Keep your mouth closed. Let your teeth rest lightly together and your tongue touch the center of the roof of your mouth. The aim is to be completely free of tension, but not to be so relaxed that you fall asleep. Wear clothes that feel comfortable, and do make sure that, while meditating, your legs and lower body are covered.

4 *Rhythmic chi*
How to Breathe

Start by taking slow, deep breaths. Take the same time to breathe in and out – if you breathe in to a count of ten, you should also breathe out to a count of ten. Make your breathing calm and regular. Breathe quietly and bring your attention to the inflow and outflow of breath. When you have reached a feeling of comfortable relaxation, you can begin to turn your attention to the object of your meditation.

Always sit comfortably when meditating for good chi flow. Try sitting cross-legged in the half-lotus position with the sole of one foot facing upwards and, in time, progress to the full lotus with both soles facing upwards.

DEEP BREATHING

You can either use breathing techniques prior to contemplative meditation or engage in breathing as an end in itself. The latter practice is best undertaken under instruction from a qualified teacher, as it develops the yoga of breathing and can be highly powerful. You can, if you wish, try holding in your breath for up to five seconds,, then breathing out. Practice this regularly until you can do it with ease.

The art of tea drinking

"The first cup moistens my lips with pleasure; the second cup soothes my parched throat; the third cup assuages my loneliness; the fourth cup calms my inner fire; the fifth cup purifies my spirit; the sixth cup clears my mind; the seventh cup takes me to the realms of the Immortals."

or more than a thousand years, tea drinking has given great pleasure to the Chinese – it is the drink most lavishly praised, even above wine. Tea symbolizes earthly purity, so its preparation calls for the most stringent standards of cleanliness. From the moment they are plucked, dried, and stored, to the time when they are prepared for drinking, the highly prized tea leaves are kept with the greatest care.

To the Chinese, drinking tea is associated with a special preparation ritual, which allows the mind to settle and become mellow, so it is never drunk in the company of rowdy friends. You cannot enjoy good tea when there are noisy children nearby or people quarrelling or shouting in the next room. Tea drinking is regarded as a civilized activity to be enjoyed in quiet company and in an atmosphere where there is no unbridled showiness. It connotes subtlety and an under-stated, almost reclusive atmosphere. Tea should never be viewed merely as a means to assuage thirst. It is a means of enjoying quiet camaraderie and relaxation. Conversation is often subdued, and those who enjoy a good cup of tea may have little to say. Instead, there is relaxed contemplation and a serene feeling of companionship. The serious tea drinker is almost always a philosopher of sorts, and connoisseurs who appreciate the art of tea drinking are usually passionate – in a quiet, understated way – about the paraphernalia used and the ritual to be observed.

PREPARATION

Vital to the preparation ritual is the use of two well-made teapots: one for preparing the tea and for keeping the tea leaves moist, but not soaked in water; the other for containing the freshly brewed tea. The water used must always be adequately boiled and teacups always properly warmed before use. In fact, the art of boiling water for tea has been developed and refined to unbelievable perfection, and the whole ritual has an almost Zen-like quality.

Teapots should, preferably, be made from a special clay that is fired to a brick-red color, is hard (almost like stoneware), yet soft enough to crumble under a sharp steel blade. The texture of the pot must allow it to "breathe." The ideal teapot holds three small cups of tea. A perfectly made teapot will have its spout, lid, and handle resting in equilibrium when the pot is overturned. New teapots must always

Tea drinking is an important art in China. It is not a rowdy occasion, but one where the tea is greatly appreciated and where relaxed, contemplative conversation takes place.

Black tea that has grown wild on a rock terrain is considered one of the best types to drink. Spring water is thought to give the best flavor to the tea.

be "seasoned," with tea leaves soaked in water boiled to high temperatures, prior to being used. This is to remove any lingering odors of clay.

Most important, of course, is the quality of the tea leaf itself. There are different types of tea, and selection is always a matter of choice and the size of your purse. The best teas are said to be black teas, but the paradox is that the best-quality black teas never look black but instead a slightly yellowish-green (not to be confused with the lower-grade green tea). Tea grown on rocky terrain on hilly land is said to be superior to tea grown on the plains. Tea that grows wild (as opposed to being cultivated) is said to be the most highly prized. Tea grown in the Fujian province of China has been famous for centuries, so it is said that the best-quality tea comes from here.

The choice of water for making the tea is also considered to be important, since the wrong kind of water can destroy the subtle flavor of tea. Spring water that is pure and flows fast is considered good, as is water taken from wells that are used daily. In cities, there is, of course, no choice but to use piped water, although I know die-hard connoisseurs who use genuine, pure bottled spring water and who even prefer water that has been boiled by charcoal to electrically or gas-boiled water (although personally I have found there to be little difference).

THE TEA RITUAL

The ardent tea drinker will explain to you that water takes three stages to boil: the first stage is when tiny bubbles occur; the second is when bigger bubbles appear; and the third is when steam is emitted. As soon as this happens, lift the kettle from the heat to ensure that the water does not get overboiled. Finally, the kettle used for boiling the water should be earthenware rather than metal. This is not easy, however, and many tea connoisseurs have now resigned themselves to accepting the metal kettles of today.

When water in the kettle has reached the third stage of boiling, pour it into an empty teapot to warm the pot and then wash the teacups with the boiling water. Next, empty the teapot and put in the tea leaves. Remember not to block the spout, as doing this is said to bring inauspicious luck to the tea drinker. Fill the teapot about halfway with tea leaves (some people even make it three-quarters full). Next, pour the boiled water into the teapot until the water overflows. Quickly pour away this water to "cleanse" the tea leaves. Make sure that you drain away all of the water. It is only when you use the first infusion to clean the tea leaves of dust and impurities that you will get the real taste of the tea. Otherwise, there is the danger of it leaving behind a bitter aftertaste.

*T*he second infusion of the tea is the real thing. Pour boiling water into the teapot along the edge, until once again it overflows. Replace the lid and then give the lid and the whole teapot a splash of boiling water as well. In a matter of a few seconds, the tea will be considered to have been "adequately prepared for drinking," and it can now be transferred into a second, more lavishly decorated, teapot. Drain all the tea into this second teapot, making certain that the tea leaves in the first teapot remain wet but are not soaking in water. Now you can pour the tea into little teacups. How good it tastes depends on how expert you have been in preparing it!

You should drink tea as hot as you can bear it, as this is when it tastes really good. Bring the teacup near your nostrils to savor the aroma of the tea. When you have finished the first cup, wash your cup with boiling water and prepare another infusion by repeating the brewing process all over again. Tea is best enjoyed after a hearty meal and should never be drunk on an empty stomach.

The basic principles of tea drinking are cleanliness, the use of proper utensils, and good technique. A relaxed, contemplative mood should prevail and there should not be more than a few people around. Drinking tea is not the same as drinking wine, so it cannot be enjoyed in hot, damp, or stuffy rooms, but is best appreciated while looking at art, listening to music, reading poetry, or engaged in philosophical conversation.

Good tea will usually have the effect of clearing any feelings of languor or drowsiness that you may be feeling and it is a good idea to precede meditation sessions with a short tea-drinking ritual. This signifies purifying the physical body prior to entering into the realm of spiritual consciousness through meditative yoga and visualization.

Basic
buddhist wisdom

The Chinese view of life, and of the human role within it, has been extensively colored by Buddhist beliefs. A popular legend from China, which bears the title "Journey to the West" (and which as a child I was told many times), describes the odyssey of a humble monk accompanied by his two companions, the monkey and the pig, who travel with him in search of precious Buddhist scriptures.

Opposite: Buddhist beliefs have greatly affected the Chinese way of life. Shakyamuni Buddha was a prince who was descended from "enlightened beings." He taught that life and death are ruled by karma, and that there is a continuous cycle of birth and rebirth known as samsara.

The footprints of Buddha are popularly used as sacred symbols in Buddhist art.

A long the way, they are accosted by demons and temptresses, who make unsuccessful attempts to distract them from continuing their journey. Aided by the wily monkey, the monk eventually arrives in the presence of the Buddha, whose great compassion overwhelms him. He accepts the scriptures from Buddha and travels back to China, now blissfully in possession of the sacred teachings. Alas, along the way he stumbles while crossing a river and portions of his precious texts drop into the raging waters and are carried to the countries of Thailand, Cambodia, and Burma.

It was this karmic accident that caused the scriptures that were brought back to China to be incomplete – or so it has been postulated. This also explains the differences between the Buddhism that is practised in China and that practised in Thailand, Cambodia, and Burma. Nevertheless, despite superficial discrepancies, the fundamental wisdom of Buddha's teachings remains intact in all Buddhist traditions.

THE TEACHINGS OF SHAKYAMUNI BUDDHA

No book on Chinese wisdom would be complete without a description of the historical traditions and basic beliefs of Buddhism. Shakyamuni Buddha was a prince from a small northern Indian state. He was neither god nor mythological figure, but a man, albeit a most extraordinary man – one of an endless line of "enlightened beings."

Shakyamuni Buddha taught that the universe is timeless; it has no beginning and no end. Life and death are governed entirely by the law of karma, and man's existence is a never-ending cycle of birth and

rebirth, known as samsara. The quality of this rebirth (and which of the Six Realms of Existence you are reborn into) is determined by your karma – the law of cause and effect. It is karma that gives life its moral code. Buddhism, therefore, advocates living with a good heart to create positive karma.

Four important mental states are stressed. Called "the immeasurables," these are the states of:

● Developing immeasurable mental equanimity – remaining tranquil and unattached
● Developing immeasurable loving compassion for the suffering of all beings
● Developing immeasurable joy in the happiness of all others
● Developing immeasurable love and the wish for a good rebirth for all living beings.

Buddhism does not believe in a supernatural power or an omnipotent god. Salvation does not come from the intervention of a divine entity. Rather, Buddhism advocates the practice of compassion and loving kindness towar all living beings, combined with meditation practices to develop wisdom. Prayers to the Buddhas are a supplication for blessings to give one the wisdom to understand the true nature of reality. Attainment of enlightenment is a state of mind that generates perpetual bliss through spontaneous compassion.

All Buddhas are, therefore, said to be most kind and compassionate. Every living being is said to possess the imprint of Buddha nature. It is through living a moral life, practising compassion, and meditation that this imprint can be developed to high levels of attainment and wisdom, which in turn leads to enlightenment.

THERAVADA AND MAHAYANA BUDDHISM

There are two main schools of Buddhist practice: Theravada and Mahayana. The tradition practised in China is Mahayana Buddhism, but both schools focus on the Four Noble Truths and the Eightfold Path. Theravada Buddhism emphasizes breaking out of the cycle of birth and rebirth – called "liberation from samsara." Mahayana Buddhism emphasizes liberation as well as the attainment of enlightenment for the sake of helping all beings. It stresses the need to cultivate benevolent motivations toward all living beings; to have compassion and love for others; and a selfless, altruistic attitude, which is paramount before you are able to attain enlightenment.

THE FOUR NOBLE TRUTHS ARE:

1 All existence is suffering
2 The causes of suffering arise from your own mind (attachment, anger, and ignorance)
3 All suffering can cease and be rooted out
4 The way to cease all suffering is to follow the Eightfold Path.

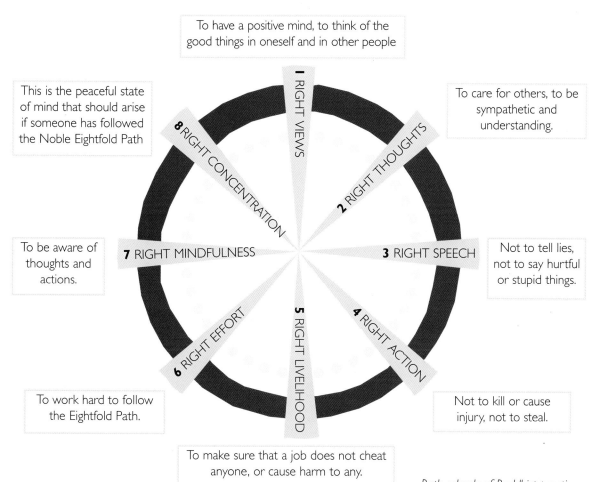

To have a positive mind, to think of the good things in oneself and in other people

To care for others, to be sympathetic and understanding.

This is the peaceful state of mind that should arise if someone has followed the Noble Eightfold Path

Not to tell lies, not to say hurtful or stupid things.

To be aware of thoughts and actions.

Not to kill or cause injury, not to steal.

To work hard to follow the Eightfold Path.

To make sure that a job does not cheat anyone, or cause harm to any.

1 RIGHT VIEWS
2 RIGHT THOUGHTS
3 RIGHT SPEECH
4 RIGHT ACTION
5 RIGHT LIVELIHOOD
6 RIGHT EFFORT
7 RIGHT MINDFULNESS
8 RIGHT CONCENTRATION

The Eightfold Path

Both schools of Buddhist practice, Theravada and Mahayana, follow the stages of the Eightfold Path. The Wheel shown here represents these teachings of the Buddha. When a high lama gives a teaching, he is said to be "turning the Dharma Wheel."

In all, there are said to be 84,000 recorded teachings of the Buddha's words, and today Buddhists of all traditions strive to keep his teachings uncorrupted and true to the original Sanskrit texts. Tibetan Buddhists, for instance, are especially mindful that the words of the Buddha can be traced back to their original source. Teachings given by highly realized beings, such as the high lamas of Tibet or the master abbots of Buddhist temples in China, are considered extremely valuable, because the words of Buddha have been carefully passed on from one realized master to another down the centuries. Like a bright lamp guiding us on a dark night, Buddha's words hold out the promise of permanent happiness and eternal bliss.

Setting up an altar:
the household shrine

The daily ritual of meditating at your household shrine holds out the promise of bringing about an attitude of mind that attains the stunningly simple and spiritual realm – a precursor to the bliss of permanent happiness.

"The arrangement of altars should be as simple as possible, but also beautiful."

*I*f you are a Buddhist, it is good to set aside a small private area in your home in which to build a household shrine. Chinese tradition holds that the wise person should always strive to maintain purity of body, speech, and mind, and meditating in a private holy place at home, which incorporates the image of any of the Buddha "enlightened beings," enables you to practise such ritual purity.

The deities placed on your altar might be: Shakyamuni, the historical teaching Buddha; Maitreya Buddha, or the future Buddha; Amitabha Buddha; or, as is most often the case, the Compassionate Buddha, also known as the Goddess of Mercy, Kuan Yin. There are other Buddhas, but these ones are the most popular and well-known.

PREPARING YOUR ALTAR

Ideally, a home altar should be in a small room on the uppermost floor of your dwelling. If this is not possible, then a quiet corner of any room is acceptable. From a feng shui viewpoint, the best corner for an altar is the north-west corner, which signifies heaven. If this is impractical, then another position much favored by feng shui masters is the area of the home that directly faces the main front door. Many masters maintain that when a holy Buddha image faces the main door, any chi entering the home instantly turns benevolent. I have an altar in the vicinity of my main door precisely for this reason, but I also have another small altar where I am able to do my meditation practices.

Wherever your altar is located, it should be kept clean, uncluttered, and free of disturbances. A high altar table is ideal, but not essential.

If you cannot afford a table, shelves will do just as well. The rule of thumb is to have your table or shelf high enough so that all Buddha statues placed on it are higher than any person standing upright in the vicinity of the altar. This also applies to any pictures or scrolls hung on the wall behind.

Placing holy objects at a lower level or, worse, on the floor is to show disrespect and is considered most offensive. Remember that sacred objects are symbols of high spiritual aspirations and their purpose is to inspire the deep reverence that is necessary to enable spiritual attainment to take place.

The arrangement of altars should be as simple as possible, but also beautiful. Place your Buddha image in the center, and if possible have a light shining down on it. If your altar is to the Compassionate Buddha, place an image of Kuan Yin there. Next to the main Buddha statue you can place images of other Buddha deities.

The most important parts of an altar are the offerings placed before the Holy Object. To Buddhists, the Buddha statue is a holy object that symbolizes the holy body of the Buddha. Offerings of water, flowers, food, incense, and perfume are part of the meditative prayer ritual of the devotee's daily practice. Below is an image of Shakyamuni Buddha; his hand mudra is that of touching the earth.

It is most important to leave enough space in front of the holy objects to display sacred offerings to the Buddha. The placement of fresh offerings to the deities is a vital part of the ritual. To start with, there are five basic offerings, known as the wu kang, that are traditionally placed in front of the altar. These offerings are light, water, incense, food, and flowers, explained as follows.

1 *Light offerings*

These are usually made in the form of candles, oil, or butter lamps, although recently I have been advised that flickering Christmas lights are excellent, as these represent "millions of light offerings," with each flicker being a new offering. When lighting a candle with a match, do not blow out the naked flame with your breath, since your breath is deemed to be impure. Instead, always extinguish any naked flame in front of the altar by using your hand to waft the flame. Those whose observance of altar ritual is strict even go so far as to cover their mouths with a cloth, to ensure

that their impure breath is not inadvertently directed to the altar offerings or the Buddha image.

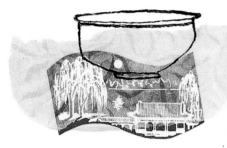

2 Water offerings

These should usually be made in seven water bowls, and the more valuable these bowls are, the more auspicious your offering will be. If you can afford it, use seven water bowls made of gold; if you cannot, then silver or steel water bowls (with or without gold plating) will do just as well. Some people use decorative ceramic bowls and these are quite acceptable. There is a ritual to making water offerings, and fresh offerings should be made each morning.

Fill a jug with water and soak some saffron in it to turn the water yellow. This symbolically transforms the water into nectar. Ensure that empty water bowls are never placed on the altar face upward, since they signify poverty due to "dependent arising." Always wipe bowls clean of the previous day's water, using a fresh cloth, and then further purify them by using incense over the inside of the bowl. As you do this ritual, say OM AH HUM under your breath. This completes the cleansing of the water bowl each day.

Pour the specially prepared saffron water into the bowls and make sure that they are filled to the brim, without spilling any water. Position the bowls close to one another in a straight line, but separated from each other by a space equivalent to a grain of rice. As you pour the water in, say OM AH HUM under your breath. This ensures that the offering of water is pure. At the end of the day, remove the water, wipe the bowl dry, and purify it with incense. Place the bowl upside down on the altar, and start again the next morning. Making water-bowl offerings is said to be most meritorious.

3 Incense offering

Place some fragrant incense on your altar. If you already have candles or lights placed there, then it is not necessary to burn the incense — having it on the altar is usually symbolically adequate. If you do burn the incense, make sure that you have a container that is large enough to catch the ash as it falls. Clean the altar daily, as a pure altar is vital to your state of mind. One of the most auspicious incenses to use is sandalwood incense. Always say OM AH HUM as you place the incense on your altar.

Different offerings can be made on your altar: light a candle, use seven water bowls, burn some fragrant incense, leave out some food such as fruit or candy, and add some fresh flowers.

4 Food offerings

These usually take the form of fruits, dates, all types of candy, and cookies. Food offerings symbolize your material wealth and it is a good idea to change the offerings regularly. Again, when you place these offerings on your altar, say OM AH HUM under your breath. This ensures that wandering spirits do not defile the food offerings on the altar.

5 Flower offerings

Flowers make the most delightful of offerings. Always use fresh flowers, for dried or fake flowers are most unsuitable. And remember that the best colors for altars are yellow and white, although blue and pink are also acceptable. Do avoid bright-red flowers, as these are deemed most unsuitable (red flowers generally being regarded as inauspicious). And stay away from flowers that have thorns. The best flowers for altars are chrysanthemums. Again, always say OM AH HUM as you place the flowers on your altar. Remove them as soon as they show signs of fading and never allow decaying flowers to remain on your altar, as this is most inauspicious.

On special holy days, which are always indicated on Chinese calendars, the offerings on your altar can be doubled or even tripled. There are also certain days when the merit gained by making these offerings is multiplied millions of times.

Meditations done in front of a holy sacred object, especially one that has been properly consecrated, enhance the chances of attaining spiritual realization. When your altar is also well kept and clean, the space is deemed to be physically pure, so meditations done here have the potential to be extremely effective.

The ritual of making prostrations

"Reverently I prostrate to the Guru Triple Gem, and take refuge in the Buddha, the dharma, and the sangha."

This is the prayer that accompanies the daily ritual of prostration. The immense merit of making prostrations to holy objects and to the Buddhas derives from an ancient ritual that has a great deal of meaning to Buddhists. There are said to be many benefits from making prostrations, and Chinese Buddhists who are serious about their practice usually observe this ritual each morning and evening. The main benefit is that prostration purifies all negative behavior arising from arrogance, pride, and vanity. It is an excellent way of reminding yourself to maintain the decorous and humble demeanor that is conducive to wisdom arising in the mind.

I have been told by my own guru, Lama Zopa Rinpoche, that "for every pore of your body that touches the ground," the merit is thousands of times greater than the grains of sand in the Ganges River. Rinpoche also told me that making prostrations is an excellent means of slicing through false pride and reducing delusions concerning your own ego. It is, in fact, particularly relevant to the modern world, where the tendency to grow arrogant is so prevalent.

METHODS OF PROSTRATION

Each morning, do at least three prostrations and, as you do them, meditate on the humble qualities of the Buddha. If possible, do three prostrations to each Buddha statue or holy object on your altar. Each evening, do at least three prostrations, chanting any purifying mantra that you know. Then meditate on all the things that you did during the day and generate infinite regret for those moments when you allowed anger to get the better of you. Feel regret also for any negative action or speech that you made during the day. This daily ritual is excellent for transforming your mind and letting you live in a state of mindfulness, which is so beneficial in helping you to attain blissful serenity.

1 Place your palms together, bending the thumbs inward; hold your joined hands at the top of your head, pointing upward.

There are two types of prostrations: the short prostration and the full, long prostration. To perform the short prostration, first place your palms together (this is described as the "prostration mudra") at the level of your forehead, then at throat level, and then at the level of your heart, then kneel down and bend forward so that your hands rest on the floor, with your palms facing down; now touch the floor with your forehead. Stand up again and repeat the ritual three times in succession.

The full, long prostration is more elaborate and requires more space: Prostrations are usually very graceful once you have learned the correct way to do them. It is important not to rush through the ritual and not to stay on the floor for too long. Everyday consistency is the key to success. Buddhist monks who are serious practitioners of the

"For every pore of your body that touches the ground, the merit is thousands of times greater than the grains of sand in the Ganges River."

 Hold your joined hands at forehead level, then at chin level, and then at heart level, still pointing upward.

3 Drop your knees and hands – palms down – to the floor.

dharma make prostrations throughout their lives every morning and evening. These master yogics are often also very skilled in the martial arts or kung fu, and great adepts of chi kung.

Tibetan high lamas require their students to perform 100,000 long prostrations as part of the preparations for receiving instruction in the secret practices of Vajrayana (often referred to as tantric

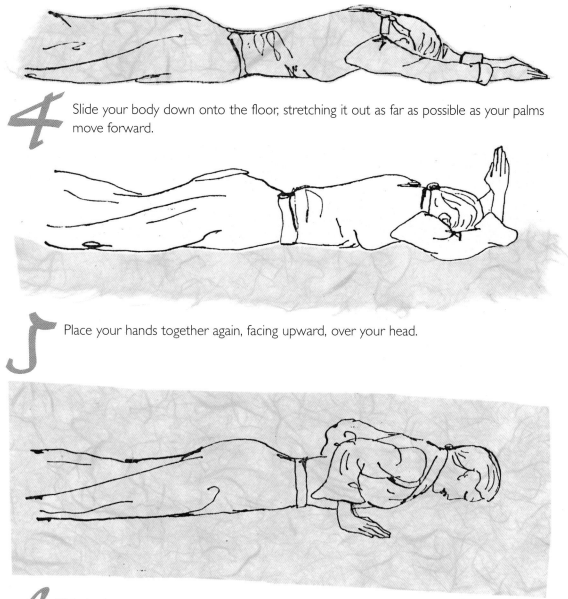

4 Slide your body down onto the floor, stretching it out as far as possible as your palms move forward.

5 Place your hands together again, facing upward, over your head.

6 Slide back to a kneeling position, pressing the floor with your palms, and then stand up. Return to your original position.

Buddhism). The Chinese believe that making 100,000 prostrations to the Compassionate Buddha, Kuan Yin, has enormous merit, since this is a powerful invocation to the Buddha, who is the embodiment of wisdom-compassion energy. The merits from performing this ritual will have lasting results, especially when done with full concentration and sincerity, and will cause the practitioner to develop a very good and kind heart indeed.

Mantras, hand mudras,
and mandalas

"I go for refuge to the Buddha,
I go for refuge to the dharma,
I go for refuge to the sangha.
May the Compassionate Mind grow
within me, and never decline."

At least once a day, Chinese Buddhists repeat this mantra in audible form - a chant that always includes an invocation for blessings to develop a good heart, together with expressions for the welfare of all beings. The original mantra, in Chinese, Tibetan, or Sanskrit, sounds incredibly beautiful when spoken aloud, and the tune to which the words are sung or chanted is hauntingly inspiring. It is not easy to convey its beauty in an English translation.

The Chinese custom is to stand before the Buddha image with your hands in the prostration mudra (palms placed together at heart level), chanting the mantra, and then making prostrations with the forehead touching the ground (see p. 143) before the verse ends.

Mantras are expressions of reverence and praise, made to the Buddha and repeated again and again. Performed with prostrations in front of a holy object, they are said to bring about a transcendence that is quite magical. Mantras should, ideally, have been transmitted by a high lama, as this gives them added potency. The words of most mantras are very simple and sound especially beautiful when they are transmitted to you in the original Sanskrit.

The most famous mantra today is probably that of the Compassionate Buddha (or the Goddess of Mercy), Kuan Yin – or Kuan Shih Yin Pu Sart, to give her her full title in Chinese. When chanted 100,000 times, this mantra will awaken the Buddha nature inside you, causing you to become more patient, kind, and gentle. It is like a direct call to the goddess and you can chant it any time you need help and feel you have nowhere else to go. Kuan Yin always answers prayers, so if you have a pressing need for divine intervention, try chanting her mantra: OM MANI PEH MEH HONE.

The words of this Sanskrit mantra pay homage to the Compassionate Buddha. Besides being suitable for use in healing practices, they are also extremely powerful for stilling the mind; for developing fearlessness in the face of danger; and for overcoming the negative impact of bad actions.

Intone the words slowly and carefully. You can pronounce the mantra any way you wish and to whatever tune pleases you. My suggestion is to make it a practice to chant this mantra 108 times each morning and evening. Use prayer beads called a mala to count the number of mantras you are chanting each day. There are three types of mala – one with twenty-one beads, one with twenty-eight beads and one with 108 beads. Give yourself a year to complete 100,000 mantras.

Remember that the mantra is there to help you induce stillness of mind, so never feel stressed about these spiritual practices. If you forget to chant the mantra one day, simply make up for it the next day. Never belittle your own efforts – as long as you chant with sincerity and the right motivation, then the mantra will be very powerful. It is, however, unnecessary to talk about your practices with others.

Prayer beads known as a mala with different numbers of beads can be used when you chant your mantras in the morning. If you use the Kuan Yin mantra, say it 108 times every morning and evening.

When you have done a reasonable number of repetitions over, say, a period of three months, it is a good idea to consider moving on to the next stage, which is to enhance your fervor while chanting the mantra and simultaneously visualizing the Goddess of Mercy seated on an exquisite throne in the space in front of you. Visualize receiving nectar and white light from the goddess. Think of the white light eliminating all your troubles, problems, depressions, and frustrations.

If you are fortunate enough to receive other powerful mantras from a high lama or a fully qualified monk, do not forget that they are powerful utterances and that their verbal meanings may elude you. So always make certain that you are chanting a mantra that comes from a source known to you. Mantras are not magical spells, but their effect may be so spectacular as to make you suspect that they are.

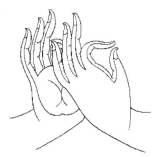

The Dharmachakra mudra, which signifies the teachings of Buddha.

MUDRAS

*M*udras are sacred hand gestures and, like mantras, when they are transmitted to you by a highly qualified guru, they take on immense psychic powers. If you look at Buddha statues carefully, you will find that different Buddhas are depicted with different mudras. This is a good way of recognizing the large number of deities in the Buddhist pantheon.

The Buddha Mudras

Here are six different mudras of the Buddha:

1 Calling the earth

This is the mudra of touching the earth, or calling the earth to witness the teachings.

2 Giving
This is the mudra of charitable giving.

3 Meditation

This is the mudra of meditation, with the left hand below and the right hand above.

4 Strength

This is the mudra for eliminating fear; Buddha gives strength.

5 Teaching

This is the mudra of teaching (very similar to number 4, except that here the thumb and index finger of the right hand are touching to form a circle).

6 The wheel

This is the mudra of turning the wheel of dharma, the teachings of Buddha.

AN ADVANCED MUDRA RITUAL

*F*or the Buddhist practitioner, hand mudras are important as part of the offerings ritual. Here mantras and mudras are combined with visualizations to make different types of offerings. When engaging in this rather advanced ritual – which goes beyond the altar offerings described earlier (pp. 136–9) – most practitioners are under the guidance of a guru. In all, there are seven types of offering: water for the face; water for bathing; flowers; incense; lamps; perfumed water; and pure food. Each of the seven offerings has its accompanying mudra and mantra. For those of you who may be interested in this spiritual ritual, here is how to perform it.

Each offering is preceded by a mudra, made by crossing the right wrist over the left in front of the breast so that the fingers of the right hand point towards the left shoulder and those of the left hand towards the right shoulder. Now simultaneously produce a clicking sound from each hand by pressing the tips of the middle fingers hard against the tips of the thumbs and bringing them down forcefully to smack against the palms.

Now perform the mudra and chant the mantra of the respective offerings. Immediately after each offering make the same clicking gesture, but this time crossing the left wrist over the right.

"Mantras are not magical spells, but their effect may be so spectacular as to make you suspect that they are."

1 *Water for the face*
OM ARGHUM AH HUM

Hold your hands out at breast level to form the likeness of a shallow bowl. Part of the rim consists of the thumbs resting upon your gently curved fingers. Chant the mantra as you make the hand gesture.

2 *Water for bathing*
OM PADYAM AH HUM

Hold your hands out separately at breast level, each with the first two fingers extended outwards and the other two fingers held down by the thumb. Then revolve the pointing fingers of each hand around the other hand three times to suggest moving water.

3 Flowers
OM PUSHPE AH HUM

Hold your hands palm-to-palm at breast level in an attitude of prayer, but with the fingers interlaced to form a single line of upward-pointing fingertips. Arch the hands away from each other in the middle to suggest the shape of a lotus bud. The thumbs should rise vertically side-by-side to enclose the near side of the bud.

4 Incense
OM DHUPE AH HUM

Hold your hands back-to-back at breast level, with the upward-pointing fingers interlaced and the thumbs held close to the forefingers to suggest incense rising.

5 Lamps
OM ALOKE AH HUM

Hold your hands out at breast level, with the palms upward and separate from each other. Curl your fingers tightly inward, so that your fingernails are pointing down, with their surfaces facing the breast.

6 Perfumed water
OM GANDHE AH HUM

Hold your left hand out horizontally at breast level, with the palm upward, the fingertips pointing away from the body and the thumb curved to rest on the palm. Hold your right hand vertically, with the thumb curved and the base of the palm resting gently on the edge of the left hand.

7 Pure food
OM NAIVIDHE AH HUM

Let your hands form a bowl, exactly as in the first offering except that your thumbs should curl inwards and rest on the palms, to suggest a shallow bowl containing food.

The above ritual is usually performed as part of holy pujas in honor of the Buddhas and in rather advanced practices. There are also simple visualizations that accompany the mudras: imagine that, in response to the first click of your fingers, an attending angel appears to receive your offering; the second click indicates that the offering has been laid at the feet of Buddha, who is now visualized as your guru or lama. To Buddhists, gurus are deemed to be manifestations of the Buddha.

This visualization ritual is extremely potent and, by performing the mudras and mantras correctly, you are said to have performed offerings of a vast cosmic dimension. If you wish, you can add one more offering to signify music, and this can be represented by a conch shell.

But how can the performance of rituals such as these aid in the expansion of wisdom? Buddhist masters have explained it to me thus. Neither the Buddhas nor the Bodhisattvas are in need of the offerings. Indeed, the elaborate mudras and mantras are nothing more than a means of generating a spirit of reverence and devotion. They are also excellent preliminaries to developing stillness of mind and purity of concentration. The more focused your mental visualization is, the more focused the concentration of your offerings will be. Eventually, with practice, you should be able to "see" jewelled bowls and fresh lotus flowers, and beautiful maidens in attendance wearing silk garments studded with jewels. It is from the Buddhist practices of visualization that the secret magic of mental imaging has become available to the world.

THE MANDALA OFFERING

In addition to the offerings ritual described above, there is another, even more beautiful ritual. This requires the use of the mandala base (the mandala being a design symbolizing the universe, usually circular in shape) and different kinds of "fillings." It involves building a mandala that is visualized as a Buddhist paradise.

As a spiritual practice, the mandala offering goes beyond time and space. It has no boundaries and its vision embraces the whole universe. The Mahayana Buddhist practice of making mandala offerings represents a means of purifying negative karma and generating positive merit. It is one of the preliminary practices that precede a meditation session.

Mandala offerings are usually performed before and after teachings by high lamas, as they signify deep gratitude for the teachings given. I love the philosophy behind the practice. There is something wonderfully sacred about generating beautiful offerings in the mind, because it focuses on an attitude of giving and appreciation.

Even if you are not a Buddhist, by sitting down to make a mandala offering to a higher presence that means something special to you, you will be engaging your body, speech, and mind and creating the means for wisdom to arise. It is useful to think through your life and concentrate on some of the motivations that made you pick up this book. Hold these motivations steady as you decide whether or not to go in search of the mandala base and learn to make a mandala offering.

The benefits of spiritual practice always manifest themselves in different ways to different people. You should, therefore, allow your personal inclinations to dictate your timing.

Eight verses of thought transformation

"One day, while out walking near the Kun Lun mountains, a young scholar met the Buddha. Overjoyed at his great good fortune, the scholar immediately asked, 'Are you God?' and Buddha replied, 'No, I am not God.' Then the scholar asked, 'Are you a supernatural being?' and Buddha replied, 'No, I am not a supernatural being.' After some minutes, the scholar asked, 'Are you an ordinary human being?' and once again Buddha gently shook his head and smiled, 'No.' Puzzled, the scholar asked, 'Then who are you?' The Buddha answered, 'I am the awakened one.'"

From an old Chinese story

Before practising the Eight Verses of Thought Transformation, first chant 108 times the mantra of the Compassionate Buddha – OM MANI PEH MEH HONE.

One of the main tenets of living taught by the "awakened one" is the practice of spontaneous kindness toward all living creatures. Kindness is just as important as wisdom. The recognition of this truth is the beginning of wisdom. Practising spontaneous kindness to everyone – irrespective of how the other party treats you – is most meritorious of all. To help cultivate spontaneous kindness toward all beings, Buddha taught the Eight Verses on Thought Transformation.

Contemplate these Eight Verses during your meditation sessions and allow the intrinsic kindness that lies within you to surface. When I was very young, my father taught me something similar. He used to call it his "eight tenets of living wisely." He explained to me that if I lived according to these tenets, I would never allow anger, frustration, or disappointment to get the better of me. Alas, these early lessons were soon forgotten, although they left their imprint on my mind.

Years later, I was amazed when I recognized the same teachings being given by my own guru. Then, in London, I attended a talk given by His Holiness the Dalai Lama, and once again the Eight Verses were being taught. These two teachings have stamped these verses indelibly on my mind and I have found them incredibly inspiring. My father was right: the verses help make the mind oblivious to the three poisons of anger, attachment, and ignorance, instead causing the rise of spontaneous feelings of kindness and compassion.

Meditating on them helps you to become awakened, to attain enlightenment. It is useful to chant 108 times (one mala) the mantra of the Compassionate Buddha – OM MANI PEH MEH HONE – before reading the Eight Verses. Visualize the Goddess of Mercy, Kuan Yin, as you chant, and request blessings to gain the experiential insights associated with these verses.

THE EIGHT VERSES

1 With the thought of attaining enlightenment for the welfare of other beings, who are even more precious than a wish-fulfilling jewel, I will constantly practise holding them dear to me.

2 Whenever I am with others, I will practise seeing myself as the lowest of all. From the very depths of my heart, I will always hold others as supreme.

3 In all my actions I will examine my mind, and the moment a disturbing attitude arises, which endangers myself and others, I will firmly confront and avert it.

4 Whenever I meet a person of bad nature who is overwhelmed by negative energy, anger, and intense suffering, I will hold such a rare one dear, as if I had found a most precious treasure.

5 When others, out of jealousy or anger, mistreat me with abuse, slander, and so on, I will practise accepting defeat and I will offer the victory to them.

6 When someone I have benefited, and in whom I have placed great trust, hurts me very badly, I will practise seeing that person as my supreme teacher.

7 In short, I will offer directly and indirectly every benefit and happiness to all beings, who are like my mothers. I will practise in secret, taking upon myself all their harmful actions and sufferings.

8 Without these practices being defiled by the stains of the eight worldly concerns, by perceiving all phenomena as illusory, I will practise without grasping to release all beings from the bondage of the disturbing, unsubdued mind and karma.

Lillian Too's afterword

I spent many happy hours poring over the images and texts included in this book on Chinese wisdom. In describing the many strands of my heritage, I have strived to present small "touches of the heart" that capture the essence of Chinese thought and attitudes — the wisdom, beliefs, superstition, attitudes, humility, and postures that color the different aspects of our traditions.

"I hope you have discovered much to delight your senses, assuage your curiosity, and touch your heart"

This book is not an academic work. It does not pretend to be an intellectual discourse on philosophical esoterica, and I ask the indulgence of scholars to consider it with compassion, especially if they judge that I may have given less emphasis to what they feel is more significant, and enhanced what they deem to be less consequential. I hope you have enjoyed the profound alongside the light-hearted — for I feel it is important to present a wisdom that embraces both the philosophical alongside the more populist folk beliefs. This is why I have investigated the deeper, reflective aspects of Chinese thinking, such as the *I Ching,* yet I have also included those beliefs that reflect the other side of the Chinese psyche: clairvoyance, fortune-telling, feng shui, and all things enticingly mystical.

As I sit with this book before me, in my mind's eye I see a yellow, radiant sun rising over the eastern horizon. At its zenith, the sun sends out magical rays that cast a golden glow over the world. Its full dazzle can be blinding, but its morning rays are soothing and gentle, like softly flowing filaments of precious yang energy. And this is how I see this beautiful book which has been put together with a great deal of loving energy. It is like an offering bowl brimming with much to delight your senses, assuage your curiosity, and touch your heart. Here, I hope I have shared with you some awesome teachings; may you, too, be inspired by them.

With all my good intentions,

Lillian Too

Kuala Lumpur, 2000.

index